Only for the Clever and Analytical Mind

Who Is Sitting on the Chair of Peter?

Volume 1

Only for the Clever and Analytical Mind

Who Is Sitting
on the Chair of Peter?

Volume 1

THE WORD
THE UNIVERSAL SPIRIT

First Edition 2007

Published by:
© Universal Life
The Inner Religion
P. O. Box 3549
Woodbridge, CT 06525
U S A

Licensed edition
translated from the original German title:
"Nür für kluge Köpfe und gute Analytiker.
Wer sitzt auf dem Stuhl Petri?" Band 1

From the Universal Life Series
with the consent of
© Verlag DAS WORT GmbH
im Universellen Leben
Max-Braun-Strasse 2
97828 Marktheidenfeld/Altfeld
Germany
Order No. S 371en

The German edition is the work of reference for all
questions regarding the meaning of the contents.

ISBN 978-1-890841-44-7
ISBN 1-890841-44-7

Table of Contents

Introduction 15

1. The dictatorship of the Holy See is based on the pagan religion of the priests. Blatant contradictions in the Old Testament 17

Do the Old and New Testaments teach "... firmly, faithfully and without error..." the truth? 19

A priesthood of pagan origin. Priests should pacify the gods. It was always a matter of external acts: ritualistic cults, magical practices, animal and human sacrifices 20

The true prophets of God as well as Jesus warned against the priests 23

Jesus of Nazareth was for the animals. He commanded that no meat be eaten, no animal be killed 25

The credibility of the books of Moses in question. Texts first written by priests during the 6th century before Christ 26

"Holy garments" for the priests, an instruction from God or a demonic insertion to secure the priests' privileges and a special position among the people? Striking contradictions to the statements of Jesus 29

Sacrificial rituals today?
Inspired by satanic energies, particularly the
great religious holidays today are unparalleled
feasts of slaughter.
Condoned by the Holy See, millions of animals
are also "sacrificed" in animal experiments 35

God, the true All-One, is always the same,
millennia ago, today, tomorrow – in all eternity.
The Church has always aligned itself with the
pagan religions of the priests, deciding
against Christ 37

Whoever contradicts the viewpoint of the Church
or of the priests "shall die." The murderous
instructions of the Old Testament still hold true
according to the Catholic Catechism and
Protestant doctrine 40

A pope undertakes the construction of majestic
buildings to "strengthen the faith of the believing
masses who look upon their glory."
And what did Jesus say? 43

The churches invented dogmas to intimidate
the people and to have a pretext for taking action
against those who deviated from them 45

The doctrines of the Church are there to uphold its
power, to impose the dictatorship of the Church 49

The way out of this dilemma:
"Come out of her, my people..." 51

2. Pagan cults of sacrifice and the priests' claim to power.
Who wrote the books of Moses?

The roots of the present-day caste of priests 53

During captivity in Egypt, the people of Israel adopted many local customs, for example, the pompous garments of the priests 57

The Books of Moses were for the most part written by priests almost 1000 years after Moses, slipping them into the Old Testament to serve their own interests and concepts 58

The priests deliberately placed themselves between God and the people. This opened the way for them to rule over the people by means of threats 60

"And God is supposed to have said that to Moses?" Descriptions from the Old Testament. Whoever does not keep the regulations "shall die" ... 62

Detailed rules concerning the priests' garments and the rituals from the Old Testament as an example for the Church today. What did Jesus, the Christ, say about the Pharisees and scribes? 65

Animal sacrifices in the Old Testament "with a pleasing odor to the Lord." Jesus always stood up for the animals 68

Only a few people know that the Holy See determines that the Old and New Testaments are "both the true word of God." It is a cruel, pagan God who predominates in the reports of the Old Testament 72

Church doctrine a crass contradiction to the true teachings of Jesus. Should the Old Testament again make a breakthrough by using the cloak of "Jesus" and "Christ"? 75

3. A work of reference for gathering information

Was Jesus, were the Early Christians, vegetarians? 81

Why did Jerome leave statements in the biblical texts that expose the Chair of Peter as anti-Christian? 82

Even a great sinner is canonized if he serves the interests of the Holy See 86

Leaving the Church – How? 87

The privileges of the priests – Cruelly instituted by the powerful 89

The reformulation of the 5ᵗʰ commandment into "You shall not murder" leaves room to justify killing 92

*The sacrificial mass – a crass and mystically
elevated practice of pagan thought in the
blood sacrifice* 93

*"Blood sacrifice" also in war? Soldiers should
sacrifice themselves for the "Fatherland."
"The canons of war" as the"speaking instruments
of the calling grace" of God?* 95

*The hypocrisy of the Catholic Church takes on
extreme forms. Popes publicly proclaim:
A praise to the Inquisition; genocide in the
conquest of South America is "a happy guilt," etc.* .. 97

*Outgrowths of institutionalized superstitions:
Black Madonnas, host pictures – "Means of
Salvation and Healing"? Crawling for indulgences –
Becoming free of sin* 100

*Doctrinal statements of the Holy See:
Absurdities and unbelievable nonsense.
Whoever doesn't believe is "excommunicated,"
damned and condemned* 105

*Shouldn't the "representative of God," at the
helm of the globe, be able to command the elements?
Jesus of Nazareth could* 107

*We need neither a Catholic nor a Protestant
Church. We need Jesus, the Christ.
The mighty Spirit of love dwells in every person* 112

4. The early Christians lived according
   to the teaching and example given
   by Jesus of Nazareth. The disastrous
   turn of development into a totalitarian
   cult of idolatry, into the Catholic Church

*The early Christians were followers of Jesus,
the Christ. They incorporated His simple teaching
into their way of thinking and living* 115

*Charismatic tasks of the early Christians in the
communities: Prophets, teachers, healers;
they lived what they taught* 120

*The "administrator" and "overseer," who took
care more of the external duties, took over the
power and became bishops and priests,
thus joining the ranks of pagan tradition* 122

*The early Christian communities lived in an
environment of idolatry, elements of which
infiltrated Early Christianity more and more* 124

*The strongly determining influence of Paul con-
tributed very decisivlely to the almost total
dissociation of early Christianity from its origin,
from the teachings of Jesus of Nazareth* 125

*Early Christianity was broken apart
through slander purposefully spread
by the caste of priests, using incitement,
persecution, torture and murder* 131

Early Christianity was turned into its opposite through the dictatorial and totalitarian power-wielding practices of the bishops 134

Emperor Constantine made what had become a thoroughly pagan church into a state church 139

We still have a state church today 147

5. The cult of Mary and revering relics: Whoever does not believe in this is eternally damned by the Catholic Church. Is a dictatorship trying to rule over a democracy? 149

The Catholic cult of Mary as the "mother of God" is deeply rooted in pre-Christian paganism 150

Mary, the virgin and undefiled woman who bore God – Whoever doesn't believe this is eternally damned. Many who pay their church taxes or tithes are not aware of this 155

Whoever does not pay deep respect and honor to the relics of the saints is damned by the Catholic Church. A cult of the dead: Belief and practice in this church is based on bones 157

Dark superstition – still today: A relic in the pectoral cross of bishops, a relic in every altar

Dogma: "Anyone who does not accept the whole of church tradition ... " – is, for all practical purposes, in hell 163

Who is sitting on the Chair of Peter? Tolstoy knew very well who had founded the Church........... 165

Protestant-Lutheran doctrine: God has pre-determined, that is, has foreseen, who goes to heaven and who goes to hell 174

A church that denies the free will of the people will deny the foundation of the legal order. A paradox in effect 176

The caste of priests determines what takes place in the state – as long as the people allow this. A dictatorship tries to rule over a democracy 179

The imperative sentence of the Catholic Church is applied in public life: "We determine what is Christian!" 181

One last word 185

Letters to the Pope 189

More information for good analytical minds about the Chair of Peter can be found under:
www.TheHolySee.cc

Introduction

Dear readers, a highly explosive book! Considering the media spectacles that are from time to time produced by the Vatican, anyone who has begun to doubt if that has anything at all to do with Jesus, the Christ, will nevertheless be outraged to find out the extent to which the teachings and structure of the Church originated directly from a pagan cult of idolatry. This cult of idolatry was enveloped with the cloak called "Christian," thus effectively duping mankind for centuries. The Church greatly interferes in the lives of individuals as well as in all aspects of public life – threatening with the eternal torments of hell all those who do not subject themselves to it. All of this has not in the least to do with Jesus, the Christ, with His simple teachings and with the original early Christianity!

Every person has the freedom to believe what he wants and every institution can teach what it wants. However, Original Christians do not remain silent when an institution abuses the name of Jesus, the Christ, by calling itself Christian, even though its teachings and deeds not only have nothing to do with the teachings of Jesus, the Christ, but even contradict them.

Regarding membership in a church, one or the other may think: "What's the harm in it?" and "At least

I'll get a proper burial!" But take care! We should not forget who is burying us and going with us on our last journey – and what it is that the representatives of the institutions are giving us to take with us into the grave, namely, eternal hell. For according to church teachings, all those who do not fulfill what the Church prescribes are eternally damned – and who does know all of it, to say nothing of fulfilling it? Even when nice speeches are made at the graveside, eternal damnation is there in the priest's subconscious and is written into church books as dogma.

In connection with this series "For the Analytical Mind – Who Is Sitting on the Chair of Peter?" how often have we heard the comment: "So what! No one knew about this!" Everyone has the chance to thoroughly inform himself about the background and interconnections of the Church. What the individual does with his newly gained knowledge is up to him alone.

In a program series that was broadcast worldwide, the Original Christians of today investigated the question: What is actually behind the Chair of Peter, also called the Holy See? How did it present itself to the people in the past? What are its intentions? And, what should we expect from it today?

This first volume of the book "Only for the Clever and Analytical Mind. Who Is Sitting on the Chair of Peter?" passes on to you the information contained in the first five radio programs.

The dictatorship of the Holy See is based on the pagan religion of the priests.
Blatant contradictions in the Old Testament

This is the first in a series of radio programs from the Original Christians in Universal Life. The Original Christians are neither Catholic nor Protestant-Lutheran, the two institutionalized churches in Germany. Instead, they are people who base themselves on Christ, who, 2000 years ago as Jesus of Nazareth, brought a very practical and ingenious teaching, the application of which leads people into happiness, freedom and peace.

Whether you, dear reader, find something in common between Jesus of Nazareth – the young man who, as a spiritual revolutionary, was a man of the people – and the Holy See with all its dusty rites, dogmas, cults and pomp, we leave to you.

If it were up to the Holy See, God would have to be silent, because already in the year 2000, Mr. Ratzinger stated in the declaration "Dominus Jesus":[1] *"… we now await no further new public revelation before the glorious manifestation of our Lord Jesus Christ."* And Mr. Ratzinger knew why he was writing this, because God, the Eternal, has never let himself be muzzled by some self-appointed representative. At all times, God has taken people and made them into His speaking instruments. And so today God speaks to all people again, through Gabriele, His prophetess and spiritual ambassador.

What does God have to say today about the Holy See? The living word of God exposes the Holy See. If you would like to, you can receive free information on this by simply writing to:

Universal Life, P.O. Box 5643, 97006 Würzburg, Germany.

Our roundtable discussions are broadcast under the title: "For the Analytical Mind – Who Is Sitting on the Chair of Peter?" Below, you will find the complete text of the first program.

The world experienced a long drawn-out media spectacle in Rome during the first months of 2005. First with the death of the former occupant of the Chair of Peter and then, with the inauguration of his successor. During the pompous festivities, the name of "Jesus" or "Christ" was discernible only sporadically. Instead, great pageantry, pomp, resplendence and riches were placed on display.

One result of such a glittering display was that questions were raised which we will try to answer: What is actually behind this Chair of Peter, also known as the Holy See, which has let itself be so continuously celebrated for so long in Rome? How did this

Holy See portray itself in the past? What are its intentions? And: What should we still expect from it?

Do the Old and New Testaments teach "… firmly, faithfully and without error…" the truth?

In addressing this question, a declaration could help us, which the current occupant of the papal chair, Mr. Ratzinger, issued in the year 2000, under the title "Dominus Jesus." In this document, he wrote the following about the Bible:

> *Taking up this tradition, the Dogmatic Constitution on Divine Revelation of the Second Vatican Council states: For Holy Mother Church, relying on the faith of the apostolic age, accepts as sacred and canonical the books of the Old and New Testaments, whole and entire, with all their parts, on the grounds that, written under the inspiration of the Holy Spirit (cf.Jn.20:31;2 Tim. 3:16; 2 Pet.1:19-21; 3:15-16), they have God as their author, and have been handed on as such to the Church herself. These books firmly, faithfully, and without error, teach that truth which God, for the sake of our salvation, wished to see confided to the Sacred Scriptures.[2]*

So, Mr. Ratzinger bases the authority of the Holy See on the Bible. Now, many people are aware of this, too, but how many people actually know what is in the Bible?

A priesthood of pagan origin.
Priests should pacify the gods.
It was always a matter of external acts:
ritualistic cults, magical practices,
animal and human sacrifices

Many of Jesus' words have been passed down in the New Testament. In Matthew, for example, we read:

But you are not to be called rabbi, for you have one teacher, and you are all brothers. And call no man your father on earth, for you have one Father, who is in heaven. (Mt.23:8-9)

From preceding verses we know it was the scribes and Pharisees who had themselves called rabbi. According to present-day usage, the scribes are today's priests, pastors, bishops, cardinals, even the so-called "Holy Father," whom we should not call Father, according to Jesus.

Why do we say this? To become a priest, a person first has to become a scholar of the scriptures, a scribe, as it were. All theologians study the Old and New Testaments and know the Bible quite thoroughly. And so, the scribes of today are the theologians, and to become a priest or minister, a person first has to be a theologian.

According to His words in the New Testament, Jesus, the Christ, was against the scribes. Why is this? Since theology is an invention of church institutions, it can be said that as a whole, God has no place in theology; instead, it is merely a work of doctrine of the Church.

Jesus himself said that the scribes closed heaven off from the people, because they constantly pointed to the work of doctrine available at that time. (Mt. 23:13) And the scribes of today point to a work of doctrine that has continued to grow over the centuries, and has become so complicated and contradictory that a person needs years just to be able to take it all in and intellectually understand it. The teaching of Jesus, on the other hand, was simple. Jesus wanted the people to develop a living relationship with God, with their heavenly Father.

Priests, scribes, and all those against whom Jesus spoke, existed even before Abraham. Since the Stone Age, early religions have cultivated ritualistic cults and magical practices. This is also true of the so-called advanced civilizations. For example, in ancient Egypt, the people revered a multiplicity of gods; and the priests, who had studied the scriptures in the writings that had been passed down at that time, were responsible for carrying out sacred acts. These were always religions of an externalized nature, in which the "god" was supposed to be appeased or made lenient through rituals. And so, these religions had nothing in common with an inner change in a person; instead they were always based on external actions.

At Abraham's time, there were special cults and festivities for the many different deities, who were believed to dwell in their temples. These, in turn, were served by human servants. And the rulers of the cities were generally acknowledged as the representatives on earth of the gods.

In Mesopotamia, the interpretation of omens and fortune-telling were important components of religion. Animal sacrifices were supposed to appease the gods and there are indications that the Phoenicians – descendants of the Canaanites – sacrificed children, often their first-born. All the rulers of the Mesopotamian region considered themselves the representatives of the gods; and the majority of their duties consisted of the practice of sacramental ceremonies that were supposed to ward off evil and bring the favor of the gods. Today we call these practices a form of paganism, of idolatry.

Usually, the centers of these ritualistic practices were the temples, although religious celebrations also took place in holy grottoes or on consecrated hills. The gods were present in these temples as statues and the priests were responsible for their care and provision. Many, many functions were carried out by the priests, such as administration, invocation, exorcism, interpreting omens, sacrifices, and so on.

The true prophets of God as well as Jesus warned against the priests

Many years after Abraham, the concept of appeasing the gods through animal sacrifices, but also through human sacrifices, was still prevalent. This is one of the reasons why the prophets of God repeatedly warned the people of Israel about the priests. For instance, in the fifth book of Moses, we read:

You shall not worship the LORD your God in that way, for every abominable thing that the LORD hates they have done for their gods, for they even burn their sons and their daughters in the fire to their gods. (Dt.12:31)

And the prophet Jeremiah said: "*The priests did not say, 'Where is the LORD?' Those who handle the law did not know me ...*" (Jer.2:8). Here, we have an indirect answer to the question of why Jesus was generally against the scribes: Because the scribes, as theologians, believed in the literal word. And yet, we read: "*For the letter kills, but the Spirit gives life.*" (2 Cor.3:6). In addition, the priests were always the ones responsible for sacrifices.

But if God did say what we just quoted from the prophets, then it is a direct contradiction to what God allegedly had said through Moses in terms of priestly robes or burnt offerings and sacrifices or animal slaughter, war and killing people. For example, Moses is supposed to have said:

Now this is what you shall offer on the altar: two lambs a year old, day by day, regularly. One lamb you shall offer in the morning, and the other lamb you shall offer at twilight. (Ex.29:38-39)

On the other hand, the prophet Jeremiah passed on the word of God with the following:

For in the day that I brought them out of the land of Egypt, I did not speak to your fathers or command them concerning burnt offerings and sacrifices. (Jer.7:22)

So at one time God allegedly said through Moses that animals should be sacrificed every day, and another time God says through Jeremiah that He never commanded any such thing.

The Old Testament is littered with such contradictions.

In another example from the Old Testament, it is written that "God" said the following through Moses: *"The priest shall dip his finger in the blood and sprinkle some of the blood seven times before the Lord in front of the curtain of the sanctuary"* (Lev.4:6).

But through Isaiah, He said: "*When you stretch out your hands, I will hide my eyes from you; even though you make many prayers, I will not listen; your hands are full of blood*" (Is.1:15). Or, for example, the following: *The Lord spoke to Moses and Aaron, saying to them: "Speak to the people of Israel, saying: From among all the land animals, these are the creatures that you may eat*" (Lev.11:1-2). And then through Isaiah, God said the exact opposite: "*Whoever slaughters an ox is like one who kills a human being*" (Is.66:3).

Since both statements cannot be true at the same time, which is right?

Jesus of Nazareth was for the animals. He commanded that no meat be eaten, no animal be killed

But what about Jesus? What did Jesus say about killing animals?

When Jesus cleared out the temple, He went through the courtyard with a whip and set free the animals that the merchants were selling for the sacrifices, according to Old Testament tradition. In Matthew, however, we read the words of Jesus: "*I desire mercy, and not sacrifice. For I came not to call the righteous, but sinners*" (Mt.9:13).

Another incident in the life of Jesus also gives a hint. Many of the disciples of Jesus were fishermen and when Jesus called them, He said: "*Follow Me, and I will make you fishers of men*" (Mt.4:19). Perhaps He was implying that in following Him, they would no longer catch fish. Certainly in many of the early Christian scriptures that are outside the Bible, countless examples are given, written in many different ways, about how Jesus stood in relation to the animals. These give witness and confirm His call to the people to eat no meat, to slaughter no animal. That these scripts are not found in the Bible is based on the decisions of the priests responsible for putting the Bible together, and not on the truth. And when we recognize that today, the pope wears a ring depicting a fisherman drawing fish onto the land, then we certainly know which point of view is favored by the Church – that which corresponds to the old conceptions of killing animals.

The credibility of the books of Moses in question. Texts first written by priests during the 6th century before Christ

But getting back to the contradictions referred to earlier, according to the Bible – which Catholic concept holds to be binding and holy – there should be no priests and no father, that is, no "holy father." But the Catholic Church has both priests and a person whom it refers to as "holy father." Of course, it could be argued that since the Old and New Testaments are allegedly holy and imparted by God, priests have existed ever since the time of Moses. In the books of Moses it is actually written that God allegedly appointed priests through Moses. This was supposed to have happened while Moses was on Mt. Sinai where he received the Ten Commandments. But did this really happen? Is this credible?

At the universities they teach theologians, that is, the pastors and priests, that a large part of the books of Moses was actually written by priests. The five books of Moses were eventually compiled from several different currents of scriptures, one of which is the so-called "P document," which assumes a priestly author because it adds material of major interest to the priesthood and from a priestly perspective. The date of the appearance of the "P document" is hotly debated among scholars, but there is general agreement that this work appeared somewhere during 770-580 BC. For all intents and purposes, they practically projected their cults, their priestly beliefs, back into the time of Moses with these writings.[3]

Most likely, influences from ancient Babylon were also contained in it, since polytheism and a caste of priests with special robes and sacrifices, prevailed in that culture.

That the books of Moses cannot have come from Moses can simply be taken from the fact that at the end of the five books of Moses we can read, "*Moses was one hundred twenty years of age when he died*" (Dt.34:7). He cannot possibly have written this line himself.

It would be interesting to examine which aspects of all the rigmarole of the priesthood in the Old Testament, which God allegedly prescribed, come up again under the Holy See today. We can draw parallels, for example, between what was allegedly prescribed and pre-determined in the Old Testament for the appointment of priests, for their vestments and for their sacrificial gifts, and how this compares with the way it is done in the Catholic Church today. And a sidelong glance at the pagan rituals on which the whole thing is based could lend considerable enlightenment to the facts of the matter.

"Holy garments" for the priests,
an instruction from God or a demonic
insertion to secure the priests' privileges
and a special position among the people?
Striking contradictions to the statements
of Jesus

What vestments were allegedly necessary for the priests can be read in Exodus:

And you shall make holy garments for Aaron your brother, for glory and for beauty. You shall speak to all who have ability, whom I have endowed with skill, that they make Aaron's garments to consecrate him for my priesthood. (Ex.28:2-3)

Can a person become holy via his garments? And if there is only <u>one</u> Holy One, and it is God, our Father, who is in heaven, then what is the meaning of such things as "holy garments"?

One explanation could be that under the outer "façade," under the magnificent robes, the person who wears these robes can hide what he truly thinks behind such a mask. The prophets have said many things in relation to this, for example, "*As robbers lie in wait for someone, so the priests are banded together*" (Hos.6:9). From this, we can deduce that what often lies behind the pointed display of such festive robes and all the rigmarole is simply naked violence.

Another aspect could be that such garments underline the special status of the person. He is raised above the masses and, with this, visibly makes known that only he can be the intermediary between God and man.

The scribes have always dressed differently than the people or even the prophets sent by God. Whoever becomes aware of what God is supposed to have said through Moses about a priest's vestments would actually have to place Jesus, the Christ, in question – because "God" is saying something quite different than Jesus, who rejected the flaunting appearance of the caste of priests. So, is the one who spoke in the books of Moses truly God or is this whole thing a demonic treatise on the prerogatives, the privileges, of the caste of priests of that time? Or was Jesus, the Christ, a false prophet? For He spoke differently than this so-called "god" in the Old Testament.

Why don't we read about what God allegedly said in terms of how a priest should dress, at the same time calling to mind how the priests of today attire themselves. This may make it easier to recognize what is behind the Holy See. For example:

These are the garments that they shall make: a breastpiece, an ephod, a robe, a coat of checker work, a turban, and a sash. They shall make holy garments for Aaron your brother and his sons to serve me as priests. They shall receive gold, blue and purple and scarlet yarns, and fine twined linen. And they shall make the ephod of gold, of blue and purple and scarlet yarns, and of fine twined linen, skillfully worked. It shall have two shoulder pieces attached to its two edges, so that it may be joined together. And the skillfully woven band on it shall be made like it and be of one piece with it, of gold, blue and purple and scarlet yarns, and fine twined linen. (Ex.28:4-8)

This text continues along these lines for several pages. Anyone who is interested can read it in Exodus, the second book of the so-called "books of Moses."

When we read this, it makes us wonder, if for no other reason than to question why Aaron and the priests should be dressed this way, while Moses himself, the great prophet, is dressed like any one of us? In this, we can clearly see contradictions between priests and prophets already beginning with the books of Moses! On the other hand, when we refer to the New Testament and read what Christ, as Jesus of Nazareth, then said to the priests at that time, He used very clear words, for example:

Woe to you, scribes and Pharisees, hypocrites! For you tithe mint and dill and cumin, and have neglected the weightier matters of the law: justice and mercy and faithfulness. These you ought to have done, without neglecting the oth-

*ers. You blind guides, straining out a gnat and
swallowing a camel! (Mt.23:23-24)*

And a little further on:

*For you are like whitewashed tombs, which out-
wardly appear beautiful, but within are full of
dead people's bones and all uncleanness. So
you also outwardly appear righteous to others,
but within you are full of hypocrisy and lawless-
ness. (Mt.23:27-28)*

This is how Jesus, the Christ, the Son of God,
spoke. And then God, His Father, supposedly said in
the books of Moses that one should dedicate holy
garments for these Pharisees and scribes?

It continues along the same vein in the Old Testament, in Exodus:

*You shall set in it four rows of stones. A row of
sardius, topaz, and carbuncle shall be the first
row; and the second row an emerald, a sap-
phire, and a diamond; and the third row a ja-
cinth, an agate, and an amethyst; and the fourth
row a beryl, an onyx, and a jasper. They shall
be set in gold filigree. (Ex.28:17-20)*

Who is speaking here? What kind of a "God" is
this, who would give such detailed descriptions of how
ostentatiously garments should be prepared for a person who will appear afterward as a priest? This is not
only odd; it is downright pagan. And even today, we
can still witness this pagan to-do, this pomp of idola-

32

try, which has nothing whatsoever to do with the word of God through the prophets of the Old Testament. And it is exactly the opposite of the word of God through His prophetess of the present time.

God, our Father, spoke very clear words through Gabriele in April 2005:

Jesus, who in the flesh was the son of a carpenter, dressed like the people. And the prophets whom I sent to the people dressed like the people. No heavenly being that ever became a human being to proclaim My message as a human being robed himself in crimson, gold and silk.[4]

It looks like much was adopted from the Old Testament concerning the priests' vestments and the whole frippery, but is it any different with the consecration of priests? In Exodus, where Aaron was commanded to slaughter, we read it described in the following way:

Then you shall kill the bull before the LORD at the entrance of the tent of meeting, and shall take part of the blood of the bull and put it on the horns of the altar with your finger, and the rest of the blood you shall pour out at the base of the altar. (Ex.29:11-23)

And yet Jesus, the Christ, in a Gospel that exists outside of the Bible said:

Verily, I say to you, for this end have I come into the world, that I may put away all blood offerings, and the eating of the flesh of the beasts and the birds that are slain by men. [5]

It has already been mentioned that through Isaiah, God said in the Old Testament: "*He who slaughters an ox is like one who kills a man ...*" (Is.66:3). With this, animal and human being are placed on equal footing: To kill life is not in the spirit of God.

And repeating what Jeremiah said in the Old Testament:

For in the day that I brought them out of the land of Egypt – precisely the time we refer to in reference to Moses – *I did not speak to your fathers or command them concerning burnt offerings and sacrifices.* (Jer.7:22)

God also announced through Jeremiah: "*Your burnt offerings are not acceptable, nor your sacrifices pleasing to me*" (Jer.6:20). And He speaks similarly through Amos: "*Even though you offer me your burnt offerings and grain offerings, I will not accept them; and the peace offerings of your fattened animals, I will not look upon them*" (Am.5:22).

Sacrificial rituals today?
Inspired by satanic energies,
particularly the great religious holidays
today are unparalleled feasts of slaughter.
Condoned by the Holy See,
millions of animals are also
"sacrificed" in animal experiments

But the question as to whether it is any different today is still open. We have seen parallels in the vestments. Is it any different today where animals are concerned? Maybe animals aren't officially sacrificed anymore in a ceremony, but where do those who like to appear on television go afterward, and what do they then eat? Even in the Old Testament, they gave God only the "inferior parts," the entrails. The priests themselves always ate the "good pieces." Has this changed today?

In the Old Testament, for instance, we read:
And the right thigh you shall give to the priest as a contribution from the sacrifice of your peace offerings. Whoever among the sons of Aaron offers the blood of the peace offerings and the fat shall have the right thigh for a portion. (Lev.7:32-33)
It seems one should make an offering of blood and fat and the priest eats the thigh! An analytical mind

will surely ask how it is today, when a reverend pastor or priest or even a high-ranking church dignitary is invited to such feasts.

At the inauguration of the new pope, a butcher gave every believer present the possibility to bring an "animal sacrifice," namely, a "Ratzinger bratwurst" – 100 grams for 85 cents.[6] And that is only the tip of the iceberg, for at the same time millions of animals are sacrificed every minute for the lusts of the palate or in experimental laboratories, which are also expressly condoned by the Holy See, that is, by today's caste of priests.[7] And the big holiday celebrations – Easter and Christmas – are the greatest slaughter feasts of so-called Christianity. Are not these a kind of sacrificial ritual? To whom are they sacrificed, these innocent animals? Who eats them? Clearly it is the priests and all those who copy them.

It is certainly not God, but rather the god of the underworld who promotes and supports such things. We can describe the god of the underworld as satanic energy, or simply as Satan. It is the adversary forces that have always tried to destroy the positive that God, the great prophets and Jesus of Nazareth brought into the world, striving to transform it into its opposite.

God, the true All-One, is always the same, millennia ago, today, tomorrow – in all eternity. The Church has always aligned itself with the pagan religions of the priests, deciding against Christ

These statements would surely trigger protests from the churches. The contradictions that we have pointed out are apparent. But the churches also teach that earlier, God commanded it a certain way, for example, in relation to the priests' garments or the rules about sacrifices, that it simply was a part of earlier times; this is how He made His will known at that time. And then, they would say, the change came with Jesus. Since Jesus, these sacrifices are no longer necessary and special garments would also no longer be absolutely necessary – although they most probably still like to wear them. For *"the Old Testament is fulfilled in the New,"*[8] so reads church doctrine, and with this, a certain continuity is guaranteed. On the whole, it is simply a change that has taken place in the will of God. This is what the churches teach, and what would most probably be given as answer.

Yet something entirely different can be read in a document of the Church. In a book entitled, "The Teaching of the Catholic Church as Contained in Her Documents," we read the following: *"For there is only one God, who created nature, who is at the helm of history and who is the author of the Sacred Books. And he cannot be in contradiction to himself."[9]*

Who is now contradicting whom? Is Jesus contradicting the Old Testament, or the Old Testament contradicting Jesus, the Christ? Then, either Jesus would be a false prophet, or God would be changeable. And if God is changeable, then He's like most people. People change. They also change their opinion every day, just as the Church endorses its own opinions, building a whole work of doctrine upon it.

But even in the Old Testament of the Bible, we read: *"For I, the Lord, do not change ...!"* (Mal.3:6).

Let us realize that if God is absolute, He cannot change. If God were to change Himself, He would be imperfect. But He is a perfect God, an absolute God. He has absolute laws. We can see that He is absolute when we look into the laws of nature. So, who is the false teacher here – the "god" in the Old Testament, or Jesus, the Christ, of our time? Or who?

An analytical mind would reach the logical conclusion that, for the most part, it is those who wrote the Old Testament. And that would be the priests, but not God.

However, in the Catholic Catechism we read something different. There it says under No. 136:

God is the author of the Sacred Scripture, because he inspired its human authors; he acts in

them and by means of them. He thus gives as-
surance that their writings teach without error
his saving truth.

And, as already mentioned, under No. 140 we can
read:

The Old Testament prepares for the New and
the New Testament fulfills the Old; the two shed
light on each other; both are the true Word of
God.

Note well – "both!" We can only conclude that if,
according to ecclesiastical opinion, the Old Testament
should be fulfilled in the New, then this invalidates
the teachings of Jesus, the Christ. For Jesus taught
something entirely different from the Old Testament.
Therefore, who is invalidating whom? The caste of
priests stands in the middle, and takes from each
whatever happens to fit its objectives. In this way,
mankind, which to a great extent believes in the caste
of priests, is ultimately seduced and led astray.

The institution of the Holy See has always referred
to those passages of the Bible that were written in by
the caste of priests, and has always been against the
statements made by Jesus of Nazareth. We only have
to think of the core teaching of Jesus of Nazareth,
the Sermon on the Mount. The caste of priests claims
it is utopian and cannot be lived. On the other hand,
such things as the robes, the splendor, the pomp,
find approval at the Holy See. Or think of the many

instructions for killing in the Old Testament and the trail of blood left by the Vatican Church over the centuries. With such a background, it follows that the Holy See has consistently favored the old pagan religions of the priests.

Whoever contradicts the viewpoint
of the Church or of the priests "shall die."
The murderous instructions of the
Old Testament still hold true according
to the Catholic Catechism
and Protestant doctrine

There is something else analytical minds could think about:

Even though Moses gave the commandment "*You shall not kill*," many instructions to murder in the Old Testament have been attributed to Moses as the word of God. For example, in Deuteronomy, God is alleged to have said:

"*... you shall put all its males to the sword*" (Dt.20:13). Or: "*I will make my arrows drunk with blood, and my sword shall devour flesh – with the blood of the slain and the captives*" (Dt.32:42). Although He gave the commandment "*You shall not kill*," God is supposed to have given the order: "*Now therefore, kill every male among the little ones, and kill every* *woman who has known a man by sleeping with him"* (Num.3:17). Credibility is impossibly strained! Such instructions may very well have been given by a demon, but never by God!

Or the following statement: *"The man who acts presumptuously by not obeying the priest who stands to minister there before the LORD your God, or the judge, that man shall die"* (Dt.17:12). Need we any other indication of authorship?

Now, an analytical mind would ask if all this is indeed to be fulfilled in the New Testament, given that the Catholic Catechism says this as a binding doctrinal statement.

The era of the New Testament is also the era of the Crusades, the Inquisition, the burning of witches. In view of these acts of violence, we can say that the Old Testament is already being fulfilled in the New Testament. They were the "human sacrifices" that were brought before the god of the underworld.

From this, we can see that the demonic energy has begun to fulfill the Old Testament in the New via the Holy See. How will this continue?

Although many may tend to dismiss this as mere words, experience teaches otherwise. Politicians, for example, take such words very seriously. In the biography of the former president of Croatia, Franjo Tudjmann, who was involved in the war in Yugoslavia, this statesman is quoted as saying: *"Genocide is not only allowed, but recommended."* [10] And he literally based himself on the almighty Jehovah of the Old Testament, although this is about present day events!

Of course, many may think: "That doesn't concern me; I am a Protestant." But Martin Luther also did not say that God is found in the inner being of a person as did Jesus. And he also confirmed the absolute authority of church teaching. He even went so far as to announce:

> *If anyone wishes to preach or teach, let him make known the call or the command which impels him to do so, or else let him keep silence. If he will not keep quiet, then let the civil authorities command the scoundrel to his rightful master – namely, Master Hans [i.e., the hangman.]* [11]

So Luther didn't bring anything new, but merely emphasized the message that whoever contradicts the Church and its teachings should be executed.

And what did Jesus say? *"Love your enemies. Do good to those who hate you"* (Mt.5:44). This is in direct contradiction to what the Catholic and Lutheran churches teach. Isn't it time Christian folk decide where they stand on this?

A pope undertakes the construction of majestic buildings to "strengthen the faith of the believing masses who look upon their glory." [12] And what did Jesus say?

But it would be interesting to know what the caste of priests thinks of its faithful. According to Reinhardt Volker in his book "Rom, Kunst und Geschichte, 1480-1650," Pope Nicholas V tried to explain this on his deathbed:

> ... particularly because the papal power is the highest, most sublime and supernatural, it requires the supporting power of the senses because the supernatural is comprehensible to most people only when their senses can grasp it. That is precisely why the papacy needs the might of structures ... What the great masses can never appreciate through a lack of education or intellectual capability, they have before them in structures ... buildings which in their sublimity seem as if erected by God, letting the sublimity and eternity of Christian teachings shine through eternally, thus producing devotio, piousness and the proper willingness to subject oneself to the head of the Church. [13]

But Jesus said: "*Do not lay up for yourselves treasures, where moth and rust consume*" (Mt.6:19). He also spoke about the fact that a human being is the temple of the Holy Spirit, and that we need no external temples; we can find God in ourselves.

Jesus, the Christ, commanded us quite simply: "*Follow Me ... Love your neighbor as yourself ... Love God.*" And He also taught: "*Do unto others as you would have them do unto you*" (Mt.7:12). This is the Golden Rule.

Jesus was a man of the people, who very simply taught love of neighbor and helped people come to recognize themselves. He encouraged them to understand where they were still at fault, and He gave them the glad tidings that with God's help they could get rid of what was not good in themselves. Thus, Jesus was a very simple man, who showed people the way to find God in their own inner being and to experience God in creation, in their fellowman, in the animals, in plants, in stones. And Jesus said: "*But when you pray, go into your room and shut the door and pray to your Father who is in secret*" (Mt.6:6). This means, link with God in you, for you are the temple of God.

So we can see that Jesus says exactly the opposite of what is taught by the Church and ultimately, by the Old Testament, as well. So who is teaching falsely? Jesus, the Christ? Or the Old Testament, that is, the "God" of the Old Testament, of which we have seen that, in reality, it is the word of the caste of priests in their writings? Again, it is the priests, who, since the times of the Old Testament, have acted against Jesus.

To lead the people astray every now and then, the caste of priests takes a few sentences of Jesus, citing from them. But only those things are picked out that fit its momentary purpose. And yet, its own teaching, the teaching of the Holy See, is supposed to be "infallible." This was established in 1870 with the dogma of infallibility of the Catholic, the papal, office of doctrine. But the statements of Jesus are like a stone quarry for the idolaters, who help themselves to them, so that the cloak of "Christian" or of "Jesus" is draped around them, thus furthering their deception of the people.

The churches invented dogmas to intimidate the people and to have a pretext for taking action against those who deviated from them

In the New Testament, the words of Jesus, the Christ, say nothing about dogmas. It would be interesting to know where dogmas come from.

The Church started them through its councils, saying: From now on this is valid as a dogma and then later, they added another one. And so, one dogma was added to the other. The last one was the physical assumption of Mary into heaven, announced in

1950, which we can read in the "Catechism of the Catholic Church" in Nos. 966 & 974. Since it is a dogma, a Catholic must believe it. If he does not believe it, then he is considered a heretic and eternal hell will be waiting for him. This is also a part of the "religious truths" that are binding. The people are intimidated and made fearful. Jesus did not say anything at all about this. He neither taught such things nor did He talk about dogmas at all.

Dogmas emerged over the centuries as the Church saw there were people who still strove for Original Christianity. One doctrine or other was then established which, in part, are very difficult to believe because they contradict common sense. Despite this, the dogmas were declared as binding doctrines and gave the Holy See an excellent opportunity to take action against those people who did not toe the church line of that time. Thus, the dogmas gave an excuse to persecute these people, to excommunicate those who deviated from the faith because they did not believe in the dogmas. From the very beginning, dogmas were used as a weapon against those who wanted to, and did, live something different, a weapon against those who would leave the Church.

This whole rigmarole was slowly put together over the centuries. Most people are not aware of this, continuing to think that the doctrine of the Catholic Church comes from early Christianity and was created on its foundation. But the facts are not consistent with this assumption, for the whole thing was built like a mosaic, piece by piece. Although many dogmas were introduced early on, they became an official part of church doctrine much later, eventually finding their way into Neuner-Roos, "The Teaching of the Catholic Church as Contained in Her Documents." (Abbreviated below as N-R.) For example, Emperor Constantine, while a pagan sun-worshipper, declared that Sunday was to be a day of rest throughout the Roman Empire in 321[14] and the Church Council of Laodicea circa 364 endorsed this by ordering that religious observances take place on Sunday.[15] Pope Gregory I (540-604) referred to purgatory as a purifying fire, but it wasn't until 1254 that it was given a dogmatic definition. (N-R 814, Letter from Innocent IV to Bishop of Tusculum) Mary as the Mother of God and immaculate conception was introduced in 649 at the Lateran Council (N-R 325), as was the Dogma of Trinity (N-R 267). Auricular confession was introduced by the IV Lateran Council in 1215.[16] The canonization of the dead was formally incorporated into church law in 1234 by Pope Gregory IX.[17] The Catholic Church as necessary for salvation (N-R 340-341) and the necessity of submitting to the Roman Pontiff (N-R 342) was introduced in 1302 by Pope Boniface VIII. Baptism as necessary for salvation was made official in 1547 at the Council of Trent. (N-R 440) The sacrament of penance (N-R 572-586) and canons on extreme unction (N-R 617-620) were made in 1551 at the Council of Trent (14th session). In 1563, invocation, veneration and relics of saints and sacred images (N-R 400-404) became official at the Council of Trent (25th session). Some dogmas were instituted quite late, during the 20th century. For example, the inspiration and inerrancy of Holy Scriptures became formal in 1920 in Benedict XV's encyclical (N-R 121-122) and Mary's assumption into heaven was adopted under Pope Pius XII in 1950. (N-R 334) The list is quite lengthy. Every century something was added to make the rigmarole ever bigger and more "beautiful."

And so, dogmas may be church doctrines, but never the laws of God. They first emerged when early Christianity had already turned into its opposite, that is, once the priests took over power.

What the Church has to say about this today, we can read in the book: "The Christian Faith in the Doctrinal Documents of the Catholic Church," by J. Neuner and J. Dupuis:

The office of authentically interpreting the word of God, whether written or handed down, has been entrusted to the living teaching office of the Church alone, whose authority is exercised in the name of Jesus Christ. (No. 248)[18]

This statement alone reflects the presumptuousness of the Church in its claim to unconditional power.

But according to the teaching of Jesus, the Christ, there is no church! For according to Jesus, there is the small chamber, into which you should go and become aware that you are the temple of God and that God is _in_ you. And the more we fulfill our prayers, by taking the commandments of God in hand as well as the teachings of Jesus, the Christ, and acting on them, the more we become a living temple. At this point, why would we need the whole hodge-podge of the Old Testament? Why would we need the whole set-up of the caste of priests, the idolaters of the present time? Jesus is the life and the caste of priests is not, whether we're talking about the Old or the New Testament.

The doctrines of the Church are there to uphold its power, to impose the dictatorship of the Church

The doctrines of the Church can be compared to the laws of a worldly state. These are made to uphold and maintain their own power. And so, in the Church's case, their doctrines are created exclusively to control the so-called faithful and to uphold the dictatorship of the Holy See. This can be seen in the fact that those who question these doctrines are punished with the highest punishment the Church can mete out. In Neuner-Roos we read what it says about doctrines:

If any one shall assert it to be possible that sometimes, according to the progress of science, a sense is to be given to dogmas propounded by the Church different from that which the Church has understood and understands – anathema sit. (No. 61)

We need only think of the scientist, Galileo Galilei, who discovered that the earth revolves around the sun. He was subjected to an Inquisition trial because of this and had to retract his statement.[19] So if we were to claim that what the Church taught back then is false today, we would be excommunicated. Clearly, these doctrines of faith have no other purpose than to uphold the power of the Church. But with Jesus, the Christ, there are no doctrines. Jesus, the Christ, was concerned with leading the people to God. Doctrines, on the other hand, serve merely to impose the dictatorship of the Church.

Perhaps the dictators of church ignorance do not take people at all seriously. Others apparently think so. Perhaps many a reader may remember the Grand Inquisitor by Dostoyevski, who also made clear to the Jesus who appeared in this story that the Grand Inquisitor and the Church had taken the teachings of Jesus, the Christ, twisted them and led the people astray with them.

And let us not forget the motive force behind Pope Nicholas V undertaking the construction of majestic buildings:

What the great masses can never appreciate through a lack of education or intellectual capability, they have before them in structures ... producing devotio, piousness and the proper willingness to subject oneself to the head of the Church.[20]

And what did we have before our eyes during the first months of 2005: majestic buildings, grand appearances, impressive music, luxury, splendor and precious stones.

The way out of this dilemma: "Come out of her, my people…"

Dear reader, can such an attitude toward the people truly be of divine origin? Or is it perhaps, rather, the expression of a satanic energy?

For those among you who are beginning to wonder how you should respond to this information, there is a way out. The way out of the dilemma, which perhaps you can discover for yourself, can also be found in the Bible where it says: *"Come out of her, my people, lest you take part in her sins, lest you share in her plagues"* (Rev.18:4).

This is only a very small part of the many, many contradictions that can be discovered when a person starts to think analytically and to raise questions, not simply accepting without criticism what is put before him.

At this point, we would also like to expressly make clear that every person has the freedom to believe what he wants. And every institution can teach what it wants. However, Original Christians do not remain silent when an institution calls itself Christian, the teachings of which not only have nothing to do with the teachings of Jesus, the Christ, but even contradict them.

Pagan cults of sacrifice and the priests' claims to power. Who wrote the books of Moses?

We have now reached the second part of the radio series: "For the Analytical Mind – Who Is Sitting on the Chair of Peter?"

The media campaign presented worldwide by the Chair of Peter at the beginning of 2005 gave impetus to this roundtable discussion of the Original Christians. We want to examine more closely the following questions: What is actually behind this Chair of Peter, also known as the Holy See? How did the Holy See portray itself in the past? What are its intentions? And, what should we still expect from it?

The roots of the present-day caste of priests

Following, we will again take a look at the roots of the present-day caste of priests in Rome with its rites and ceremonies, with its pomp, its wealth and splendid robes. These roots reach all the way back to Old Testament times. We will start with the following question: Was there such a caste of priests already at the time of Abraham?

Abraham came from the city of Ur in Chaldea, the country of present-day Iraq. The people believed in many gods, and at that time, many priests and many different kinds of cults flourished there. The family in which Abraham grew up was no different and practiced paganism, like all the families of that time. This paganism had, of course, its corresponding priests.

Abraham lived during the time of the Sumerians in Mesopotamia, which was during the first half of the 2nd millennia before Christ. And it was in Babylon that the Sumerians developed a whole world of gods. There was a sun god; there were various city gods; there was a goddess of love named Ischtar and there was also a hierarchical caste of priests who regarded themselves as intermediaries between their particular god and the people.

The rulership of the state was in the hands of the caste of priests. The king was, at the same time, the priest-king and his task was to appease or pacify the god or gods and establish communication between the people and these deities.

According to the concepts of that time, the "gods" evidently required sacrifices. They required animal sacrifices but also human sacrifices. It was not seldom that to satisfy a particular deity of that time, a firstborn child was sacrificed to it.

Isaac was Abraham's firstborn son and Abraham loved him above all things. To have a son whom he designated as his heir and placed before all his other children was for Abraham a deep heartfelt feeling. According to the Bible, it was to Abraham that God said: *"Take your son, your only son Isaac ... and offer him there as a burnt offering ..."* (Gen.22:2). With this, God actually meant that Abraham should sacrifice the strong binding he had with his son and not to sacrifice his son, per se.

Abraham struggled with God's demand that he sacrifice his firstborn, his favorite son. The word "sacrifice" was so deeply rooted in his consciousness that he actually thought God meant a human sacrifice. To Abraham the thought of human or animal sacrifices was totally normal, and that he should sacrifice a son to God also fit, because from his point of reference, from the polytheism he grew up in, he thought he was relating to a pagan god. It was clear to him that he now had to bring God a human sacrifice, his beloved son.

But this was a misunderstanding on the part of Abraham. What God did not want was that Abraham idolize his son, as we would say today, loving his son more than God. Instead, he wanted Abraham to put Him, God, in first place. But Abraham thought this "sacrifice" meant to kill his son.

That the angel intervened and held back Abraham, saying: *"Do not lay your hand on the lad or do anything to him ..."* (Gen.22:12) was a symbol. God wanted nothing more than that Abraham take his son by the hand and that both go to Him, to the one God of love. He wanted Abraham to put not Isaac in first place, but always God. And Abraham, of course, misunderstood this; he wanted to be obedient and would have killed Isaac, making such a "sacrifice." In the end, we know that Abraham sacrificed a ram, instead. However, we know through later prophets that God also spoke out against such sacrifices.

So here, too, the old pagan way of thinking still managed to come through – "if not my son, then at least an animal!" We can see that a struggle took place in the human being, in this case, in Abraham. The growing awareness of the Spirit of God, the only one God, could only gradually come to prevail against the old caste of priests and its precepts. Centuries were needed, during which true prophets appeared again and again and struggled with the pagan priest-cults over the true sacrifice, which did not consist of people or animals, but of growing into a devotion to God.

In polytheism, fear of the gods was very basic, a fear that the gods would simply attack a person and take away his animals and land, kill him, torture him and the like. In the Old Testament, we can read over and over again that God had to be appeased. So by sacrificing a ram, Abraham was also trying to appease God, along the lines of: "Please don't be mad at me if I don't sacrifice my son now. Don't do anything to me and above all don't do anything to Isaac; this is why I sacrifice this ram to you, to appease you." Even though Abraham already knew about God, the All-One, he was relating to a cruel god from polytheism, since this thought still continued to have influence over him.

During captivity in Egypt,
the people of Israel adopted
many local customs, for example,
the pompous garments of the priests

The pagan concept cultivated by the caste of priests that God is a cruel God can also be found in other books of Moses, for example, in the reports given about the time after Moses led the people out of Egypt. Moses, the great prophet, received the commandments from God on Mount Sinai. When he descended from Mount Sinai, the Israelites had built a calf of gold and were sacrificing to it. Here again, the influence of the pagan priesthood was at work, for the Israelites had just come from Egypt, and this pagan priesthood with its sacrifices had also existed in Egypt. That is where the Israelites learned about this custom. They took many customs, religious and otherwise, from the people of Egypt, which they made their own, for they had not yet developed a trust in the merciful and kind God.

This influence of the pagan religions of the priests on the people of Israel at the time of Moses is quite understandable. The Jewish people had been held captive in Egypt over several centuries, and saw how the caste of priests was clothed, what they did and what power they held. It is quite evident that much of this was adopted by the Israelites, beginning with the pompous clothing. From history, we know about the splendid, costly clothing of the Pharaohs and their caste of priests. It is quite natural to think that the Israelites would have copied this, as well.

The Books of Moses were for the most part written by priests almost 1000 years after Moses, slipping them into the Old Testament to serve their own interests and concepts

In tracing back the authorship of the books of Moses, the most widely accepted theory among non-traditionalists is the documentary hypothesis. According to this hypothesis, several documents were created over the centuries by different "authors," the predominant opinion being that many of the stories were orally passed on over the generations before being written down. One of the most influential of these is called the "P document," which assumes a priestly author because it adds material of major interest to the priesthood and from a priestly perspective.[21]

As stated earlier, the date of the appearance of the "P document" is hotly debated among scholars, but there is general agreement this work appeared somewhere during 770-580 BC. It was most probably refined and compiled by the Israeli priests living in exile in Babylon at that time. For all intents and purposes, they practically projected their cults, their priestly beliefs, back into the time of Moses with these writings. Most likely, influences from ancient Babylon were also contained in it, since polytheism and a caste of priests with special robes and sacrifices prevailed in their culture.

Thus, the books of Moses were not written during Moses' lifetime, but almost a thousand years later. Before that, there were individual records, for example, the first records about Moses go back to the time of King David and King Solomon. But there was nothing in them about these priest cults. As mentioned above, that was added later, most likely during the 6th century before Christ.

To be precise, the priests used Moses to slip their concepts, their desires, their positions into the so-called Pentateuch. In the final analysis, the Old Testament of the Bible is a product of the priests and not of Moses.

The priests deliberately placed themselves between God and the people. This opened the way for them to rule over the people by means of threats

An analytical mind would try to figure out why the priests should play such an important role. It is certainly important to the priests, because through this they can place themselves between God and the people saying: "You need priests to attain your salvation. You need priests to pacify God. You need priests to carry out everything that is prescribed, so that you are good adherents of the cult."

Today, it is very similar; the priests who stand between God and the people are important. But what did Jesus say? Jesus never spoke about priests. Instead, He taught: *"The kingdom of God is in you"* (Lk.17:21). According to this teaching, every priest, every caste of priests and every priestly institution is superfluous.

There are also well-known theologians, for example, Rupert Lay and Herbert Haag, who say that Jesus did not appoint any priests.[22] He neither founded a church, nor appointed priests. If the prophets did not want priests, and Jesus, the Christ, wants them even less, then it must be the people who want priests. But why? Can it be that it is much easier to go to a priest and confess, and then have him take away all my sins, than if I have to go to someone to clear things up with him, myself? The priest takes away the need for any effort on my part, and I get into heaven scot-free, so to speak. This is a superstition still taught by the Church today.

Apparently, people need high-ranking personalities. The all-too-human ego wants to have an image before it that represents God. But was this idea present from the very beginning, or was it instilled in the people? And by whom? Most probably by those who profit from it, namely, the priests.

If Jesus of Nazareth taught that *God is within, in you*, this had to have been a message that moved the hearts of the people. So how did the people get the idea that they needed confessionals, that they had to buy indulgences and make sacrifices? A caste of priestly idolaters would have an easy time teaching these to the people by practicing a coercion linked with spiritual threats of punishment such as: "If you do not follow us, then you will land in Hell. If you do not do what we have ordered, then you will not go to God." Here, we find repeated what was already a part of the so-called "P document," referred to earlier, namely, a certain legal order that contains very specific regulations about how the people should behave, and makes dire threats to those who do not fulfill these rules.

If the scripture of the priests was written almost a 1000 years after Moses, then we can well imagine, particularly considering those who wrote it, that what is in the books of Moses today has little to do with reality. Instead, they were cleverly colored, a thousand years later, to fit their wants.

"And God is supposed to have said
that to Moses?"
Descriptions from the Old Testament.
Whoever does not keep the regulations
"shall die"

These books should be read with the utmost caution, never losing sight of the fact that a caste of priests – the enemy of prophets, as depicted in Walter Nigg's book, "Prophetische Denker. Löschet den Geist nicht aus,"[23] – is writing about Moses here. If we question whether God really would have said something through Moses, we quickly note how improbable it is; for example, that God would have said the following through Moses:

Then bring near to you Aaron your brother, and his sons with him, from among the people of Israel, to serve me as priests – Aaron and Aaron's sons, Nadab and Abihu, Eleazar and Ithamar. And you shall make holy garments for Aaron your brother, for glory and for beauty.

You shall speak to all the skillful, whom I have filled with a spirit of skill, that they make Aaron's garments to consecrate him for my priesthood. These are the garments that they shall make: a breastpiece, an ephod, a robe, a coat of checker work, a turban, and a sash. They shall make holy garments for Aaron your brother and his sons to serve me as priests ... And they shall make the ephod of gold, of blue and purple and scarlet yarns, and of fine twined linen, skillfully worked. It shall have two shoulder pieces attached to its two edges, so that it may be joined together. And the skillfully woven band on it shall be made like it and be of one piece with it, of gold, blue and purple and scarlet yarns, and fine twined linen. You shall take two onyx stones, and engrave on them the names of the sons of Israel, six of their names on the one stone, and the names of the remaining six on the other stone, in the order of their birth. As a jeweler engraves signets, so shall you engrave the two stones with the names of the sons of Israel. You shall enclose them in settings of gold filigree. And you shall set the two stones on the shoulder pieces of the ephod, as stones of remembrance for the sons of Israel. And Aaron shall bear their names before the Lord on his two shoulders for remembrance. You shall make settings of gold filigree, and two chains of pure

*gold, twisted like cords; and you shall attach
the corded chains to the settings.* (Ex.28:1-4;6-14)

Continuing several verses later:
*You shall make the robe of the ephod all of blue.
It shall have an opening for the head in the
middle of it, with a woven binding around the
opening, like the opening in a garment, so that
it may not tear. On its hem you shall make pome-
granates of blue and purple and scarlet yarns,
around its hem, with bells of gold between them,
a golden bell and a pomegranate, around the
hem of the robe. And it shall be on Aaron when
he ministers, and its sound shall be heard when
he goes into the Holy Place before the Lord,
and when he comes out, so that he does not
die.* (Ex.28:31-35)

For an analytical mind, strong doubts would come
into play, as to whether God really did say this. It is
impossible to imagine that God would need such
pomp, such ostentatious veneration. Above all, it is
impossible to believe that a person should die merely
because he did not keep such regulations.

And yet, *"... so that he does not die"* is written
here, that is, the high priest shall be killed if he does
not wear the prescribed garment. And God, the Eternal One, spoke through Moses in the Ten Commandments: *"You shall not kill."* Such a contradiction is

Very detailed instructions are given in Leviticus: *If his offering is a burnt offering from the herd, he shall offer a male without blemish. He shall bring it to the entrance of the tent of meeting, that he may be accepted before the Lord. He shall lay his hand on the head of the burnt offering, and it shall be accepted for him to make atonement for him. Then he shall kill the bull before the Lord, and Aaron's sons the priests shall bring the blood and throw the blood against the sides of the altar that is at the entrance of the tent of meeting. Then he shall flay the burnt offering and cut it into pieces, and the sons of Aaron the priest shall put fire on the altar and arrange wood on the fire. And Aaron's sons the priests shall arrange the pieces, the head, and the fat, on the wood that is on the fire on the altar; but its entrails and its legs he shall wash with water. And the priest shall burn all of it on the altar, as a burnt offering, a food offering with a pleasing odor to the Lord.* (Lev. 1:3-9)

These words, "*a pleasing odor to the Lord,*" sound just like paganism, a pacifying of the gods by bringing them a sacrifice. The book of Leviticus is filled with instructions about sacrifices, that is, about how animals should be killed. It is even written that Moses supposedly consecrated the priests in the following way:

And Moses brought Aaron's sons and clothed them with coats and tied sashes around their waists and bound caps on them, as the LORD commanded Moses. Then he brought the bull of the sin offering, and Aaron and his sons laid their hands on the head of the bull of the sin offering. And he killed it, and Moses took the blood, and with his finger put it on the horns of the altar around it and purified the altar and poured out the blood at the base of the altar and consecrated it to make atonement for it. And he took all the fat that was on the entrails and the long lobe of the liver and the two kidneys with their fat, and Moses burned them on the altar. But the bull and its skin and its flesh and its dung he burned up with fire outside the camp, as the LORD commanded Moses. Then he presented the ram of the burnt offering; ... And Moses killed it, and threw the blood upon the altar round about. (Lev. 8:13-19)

This goes on and on with the most incredibly horrible instructions. And they always end with a sentence like: "*as a burnt offering ... a pleasing odor ... an offering by fire to the Lord ...*" Or also: "*as the Lord commanded Moses*" (Lev. 8:21).

In another passage, it describes how a turtle dove or a pigeon should be sacrificed: "*And the priest shall bring it to the altar and wring off its head, and burn it on the altar; and its blood shall be drained out on the side of the altar"* (Lev.1:15).

These cruel rituals are recorded in the book of Leviticus. It is a part of the so-called books of Moses, which at least for the most part, were written by the priests considerably after the fact. It also completely contradicts the first book of Moses where God said:

Behold, I have given you every plant yielding seed that is on the face of all the earth, and every tree with seed in its fruit. You shall have them for food. And to every beast of the earth and to every bird of the heavens and to everything that creeps on the earth, everything that has the breath of life, I have given every green plant for food. And it was so. And God saw everything that he had made, and behold, it was very good. (Gen.1:29-31)

The instructions found in Leviticus also contradict many other passages that have been cited previously. They certainly contradict the fact that shortly before, Moses had received the Ten Commandments, where God expressly commanded: *"You shall not kill."*

To round things off, one last statement about what the priests should do at the altar in honor of God, for example, the instructions to the priests on how to sacrifice doves end in the following way:

He shall remove its crop with its contents and cast it beside the altar on the east side, in the place for ashes. He shall tear it open by its wings, but shall not sever it completely. And the priest shall burn it on the altar, on the wood that is on the fire. It is a burnt offering, a food offering with a pleasing odor to the Lord. (Lev.1:16-17)

These descriptions depict a very cruel God: "*With a pleasing odor to the Lord.*" But Jesus, the Christ, taught us the God of love, the God of peace, the God of unity, the God who is with nature, for nature, for the Mother Earth.

Only a few people know that the Holy See determines that the Old and New Testaments are "both the true word of God." It is a cruel, pagan God who predominates in the reports of the Old Testament

It is quite conceivable to understand now why God, our eternal Father, sent His Son, Jesus, the Christ, to put an end to all these cults, to all this paganism. And Jesus, the Christ, did teach what puts an end to it. Then and today, He was and is against the caste of priests, which uses God as means to its own ends.

Many may now say: "But all this is long since past. It has no relevance today." But the present-day caste of priests says, on the other hand that the New Testament fulfills the Old. Doesn't this mean that at some point in time, these horrible scenes from the Old Testament will again flow into New Testament times? In the final analysis, this is what the Catholic Church decreed in its Catechism, where we read under No. 140: *"The Old Testament prepares for the New and the New Testament fulfills the Old; the two shed light on each other; both are the true word of God."*

So according to this, what we read in the books of Moses is supposed to be the true word of God. Such statements as, for example, in Leviticus 20 where we read: *"For anyone who curses his father or his mother shall surely be put to death..."* (20:9). Or: *"If a man commits adultery with the wife of his neighbor, both the adulterer and the adulteress shall surely be put to death"* (20:10). Or in a reference to homosexuality: *"If a man lies with a male as with a woman, both of them have committed an abomination; they shall surely be put to death..."* (20:13). Or also: *"If a man lies with an animal, he shall surely be put to death, and you shall kill the animal"* (20:15). And at that, even though the animal was forced into it and couldn't help itself. It then goes on to say: *"If a woman approaches any animal and has sexual relations with it, you shall kill the woman and the animal..."* (20:16).

What is also interesting is a statement in Deuteronomy:

If a man has a stubborn and rebellious son who will not obey the voice of his father or the voice

*of his mother, and, though they discipline him,
will not listen to them, then his father and his
mother shall take hold of him and bring him out
to the elders of his city at the gate of the place
where he lives, and they shall say to the elders
of his city, "This our son is stubborn and rebellious; he will not obey our voice; he is a glutton
and a drunkard." Then all the men of the city
shall stone him to death with stones; so you
shall purge the evil ...* (Dt.21:18-21)

These are only a few examples from an abundance
of terrible regulations that are contained in this book.
And among such statements, we read that anyone
who presumes to disobey the priest shall die. (Dt.17:12)

We can also read that God allegedly called for the
destruction of all enemies and to destroy everything
that was against their own beliefs.

Many try to play down the bloody passages in these
books by saying they are only myths or stories from
the distant past. However, according to church doctrine, to assume this could be a fundamental error.
Even as late as 1965, at the very famous Second
Vatican Council, where the Church was supposed to
have made a turn toward modern times, the following
was decided:

*Those divinely revealed realities which are con-
tained and presented in Sacred Scripture have*

been committed to writing under the inspiration of the Holy Spirit. For holy mother Church, relying on the belief of the Apostles (see Jn.20:31; 2 Tim.3:16; 2 Peter 1:19-20, 3:15-16), holds that the books of both the Old and New Testaments in their entirety, with all their parts, are sacred and canonical because written under the inspiration of the Holy Spirit, they have God as their author and have been handed on as such to the Church herself.[25]

It is quite difficult to believe that the Church would teach such a thing, for this doctrine is basically saying that every atrocity contained in the Old Testament is a product of the Holy Spirit. – But Jesus called for something entirely different.

Church doctrine, a crass contradiction to the true teachings of Jesus. Should the Old Testament again make a breakthrough by using the cloak of "Jesus" and "Christ"?

Why do we still have a caste of priests today that continues to act according to the Old Testament?

Did God, our eternal Father, send Jesus, His Son, who became our Redeemer, for nothing? Today, much of what the caste of priests does is against Jesus, against His teaching, and yet, they speak of

"Jesus" and of "Christ" just as the priests' scriptures referred to Moses. They quoted Moses then, and are still quoting him today. And yet, it was the priests who invented all this – one could almost call it – nonsense. God wants something else. And He announced this via the prophets of the Old Testament and especially via Jesus, His Son. Jesus taught something entirely different from what the priests of our time are doing. There is a huge difference between the so-called "God" of the Old Testament and the present-day caste of priests, and Jesus, who brought a loving Father to the people.

We can read what Jesus taught us in the Sermon on the Mount, in Matthew:
Blessed are the poor in spirit, for theirs is the kingdom of heaven.
Blessed are those who mourn, for they shall be comforted.
Blessed are the meek, for they shall inherit the earth.
Blessed are those who hunger and thirst for righteousness, for they shall be satisfied.
Blessed are the merciful, for they shall receive mercy.
Blessed are the pure in heart, for they shall see God.
Blessed are the peacemakers, for they shall be called sons of God. (Mt.5:3-9)

And Jesus said about praying:

And when you pray, you must not be like the hypocrites. For they love to stand and pray in the synagogues and at the street corners, that they may be seen by others. Truly, I say to you, they have received their reward. But when you pray, go into your room and shut the door and pray to your Father who is in secret. And your Father who sees in secret will reward you. (Mt.6:5-6)

Another passage fits with this: "*All who exalt themselves will be humbled, and all who humble themselves will be exalted*" (Mt.23:12).

And what did Jesus say about the caste of priests?

But you are not to be called rabbi, for you have one teacher, and you are all brothers. And call no man your father on earth, for you have one Father, who is in heaven. (Mt.23:8-9)

And then a bit further on:

Woe to you, scribes and Pharisees, hypocrites! For you travel across sea and land to make a single proselyte, and when he becomes a proselyte, you make him twice as much a child of hell as yourselves. Woe to you, blind guides... (Mt.23:15-16)

Or in verse 13, Jesus said:

But woe to you, scribes and Pharisees, hypocrites! For you shut the kingdom of heaven in people's faces. For you neither enter yourselves nor allow those who would enter to go in.

It seems this last expresses the crass difference between what Jesus of Nazareth taught and what is contained in the priests' scriptures of the so-called Old Testament. An analytical mind could draw the conclusion that this difference is made worse by the Church because it claims to base itself on Jesus of Nazareth and presumes to teach that the Old Testament, with these scriptures from the priests, which Jesus of Nazareth expressly turned against, is a revelation of God that is still valid today and is supposed to shed light on the New Testament which contains the teachings of Jesus of Nazareth.

Furthermore, the New Testament is supposed to shed light on the Old Testament. But how can you shed light on the Old Testament through the New Testament – through the wonderful teachings of love, of peace and of unity? Only by identifying yourself as being the "New Testament," because what we have read from the scriptures of the priests has had light shed upon it, that is, it has been fulfilled – through the present-day caste of priests, but surely not through the New Testament. So, if we look at this statement more closely, it means nothing more than that the Old Testament should make its breakthrough again. And for this purpose, Jesus, the Christ, is used – the name "Jesus," which stands for love, for peace, for unity, for nature, for the Mother Earth, for every animal!

So, who actually was Jesus? Where did He come from?

Jesus was born of Mary and was the son of Mary and Joseph. He grew up under very modest circumstances. We know that Jesus came from the tribe of David and belonged to the tribe of Judah. This is actually an interesting fact, because from it, we can deduce that Jesus was not a priest and never could have become one either, for the priests all came from the tribe of Levi and had to be descended from Aaron, the brother of Moses. But neither requirement was true of Jesus, and thus, He never could have been a priest. So, in a very real sense, Jesus truly was a man of the people.

And as a man of the people, He also taught a magnificent and wonderful law of life, which is in God and is given to all people who love Jesus, the Christ, by following Him.

As Original Christians, we see it as our task to again give all people an understanding of this, so that the wrong impression doesn't develop that simply because they drape themselves with the cloak called "Christian," the institutions should be considered as representative of His teaching.

A work of reference for gathering information

The first programs in our series "For the Analytical Mind – Who Is Sitting on the Chair of Peter?" brought quite a lively echo from our listeners. Many letters reached us that raised questions on such issues as the ritualistic ceremonies, the dogmas, the crimes committed by the Catholic caste of priests, the assets worth billions, the pagan roots and much more.

We want to answer some of these questions today.

Was Jesus, were the early Christians, vegetarian?

A listener from Germany wrote the following.
Question:
I am a vegetarian but if I talk about it with my friends, they always argue that there's nothing in the Bible about the fact that Jesus never ate any meat. How come? In your program it was stated that God never wanted the animal sacrifices described in the Old Testament, and that Jesus never wanted people to kill animals. Could you tell me more about this? Are there any books on this subject?

Answer: A church father, St. Jerome, compiled the first Bible for the Catholic Church back in 370 AD. It is generally assumed that Jerome had access to all the scriptures on the teachings of Jesus that were still available at his time. Commissioned directly by Pope Damasus I, whose secretary he was, he compiled the Vulgate, the first Latin Bible. Jerome knew very well from all his readings that Jesus did not eat meat and also taught that animals are to be loved and not killed. In a treatise on Jovinian, Jerome made a noteworthy statement to this topic. He wrote:

The eating of flesh was unknown until the deluge. But after the deluge, the poison of flesh-meat was offered to our teeth ... But once Christ has come in the end of time, and Omega passed into Alpha and turned the end into the beginning, we are no longer allowed to eat flesh. (Adversus Jovinianum)[26]

This makes it quite clear that Jesus called on the people to eat no meat, which is confirmed in the ancient gospels that were not included in the Bible. Despite this, in compiling the Vulgate – today's Bible – Jerome withheld these important aspects of the teaching of Jesus, including instead, documents that had already been falsified.

Every day, millions of animals pay with their lives for this falsification of the teaching of Jesus. Since then, and particularly with the onset of industrial farming, countless billions of animals have been subjected to infirmity and death in dark barns; it is primarily Christian nations that have mutated into meat-eaters. The consequences of this suppression of information have been unimaginable for nature, animals and for people, as well.

Many apocryphal scriptures confirm that Jesus and the apostles were vegetarian. For example, there is a booklet available entitled: "The Hidden Love of Jesus for the Animals"[27] as well as a booklet entitled, "The Bible Was Falsified. Jerome, the Church Falsifier of the Bible."[28]

Why did Jerome leave statements in the biblical texts that expose the Chair of Peter as anti-Christian?

Question:

During the first programs a passage from the book of Revelations at the end of the Bible was quoted, where people apparently are rather encouraged to leave the Church. If this is right, why was this passage left in the Bible, when the churches have manipulated so many other things in it?
And how can a person actually leave the Church? How is this done?

Answer: The passage being referred to is found in Revelations 18:4, and reads: *Come out of her my people, lest you take part in her sins and share in her plagues.* We could even say it is a call to leave the "whore of Babylon." Over the centuries, the "whore of Babylon" has come to be interpreted as being the Church, which replaced earlier Christianity. So the question is quite legitimate: How can it be that such a notable sentence was left in the Bible?

We again have to refer back to Jerome. We have just heard that he withheld some things, but on the other hand, he also left some things in, which were frowned upon by the Holy See. Jerome was of ambivalent character. He received the task from Pope Damasus during the 4th century to compile a unified text from the many existing scriptures, and already then he recognized that it would be a difficult task. In a letter to Pope Damasus he wrote:

> *Is there a man, learned or unlearned, who will not, when he takes the volume into his hands, and perceives that what he reads does not suit his settled tastes, break out immediately into violent language, and call me a forger and a profane person for having the audacity to add anything to the ancient books, or to make any changes or corrections therein?* [29]

It was quite clear to Jerome that he would have to make very individual and, perhaps even unauthorized, decisions on his own. It is important to realize that Jerome wanted to make a career for himself in the Church; he even wanted to become pope. This is why he accepted this task, even though he must have known in his heart that some things simply weren't right in his compilation of the Bible. During his earlier years, Jerome was an adherent of Origen, who wanted to bring Original Christianity back to life, and who had also seen through the falsifications of the scriptures that later became the Bible. Origen lived during the 3rd century, that is, before Jerome, who lived in the 4th century. As an adherent of Origen, Jerome was quite aware that he ran the risk of being labeled a heretic and of becoming an outcast. So he chose to follow the middle road: He left some things out, as, for example, what Jesus, the Christ, stated about the animals.

On the other hand, he left other things in that are quite noteworthy and that in later times brought people to realize that something wasn't quite right in the Bible, that the teachings and the life led in the Church did not quite agree with what was in the Bible, for example, in fact that priests exist at all. Jesus himself said: "...*But you are not to be called rabbi*" (Mt.23:8). Or the fact that the Church justifies war, while Jesus said: "... *for all who take the sword, will perish by the sword*" (Mt. 26:52). These passages and the one mentioned from Revelations were also left in the Bible.

A logical **question** to ask here is:
So, was Jerome made into a saint by the Church because he falsified the Bible and subjugated himself to the Church?

Answer: We can certainly assume this. He fulfilled a very important task for the Church, because during his time there were many, many scriptures available. There were the so-called apocryphal scripts where much can be found, for example, on Jesus of Nazareth's love for the animals. During His time, no one was saying: "This text is more important than the other." Anyone could seek out a text that he considered a true one and which he could then test with his heart by practicing it. What Jerome did was to severely restrict this possibility, creating a canon that was the only valid one as far as the Church was concerned.

Even a great sinner is canonized if he serves the interests of the Holy See

So anyone who was or is made a saint must be subject to the Catholic Church. Whether sinner or not does not really play a role, does it?

Answer: No. Jerome fulfilled the task given to him by the Church, and this eventually led to his canonization.

This can be said of all those people who were later canonized by the Church. Whether sinner or not, plays no role. What is important is that you serve the interests of the Church.

Even Emperor Constantine is revered as a saint. We will hear more about him at a later point. Constantine was a very brutal, violent person who had his own family killed, his wife and his son. He even had his closest allies killed in the most cruel way. And yet, the Church reveres him; perhaps because he created the many privileges for the Church? There are many saints who would fit in this category.

Leaving the Church – How?

One aspect from our first question was: *How can a person actually leave the Church. How is it done?*

Answer: This is probably done differently depending on the respective country. But perhaps we could give an example on how it is done in Germany: You simply take your ID card to the relevant registry office or district court and pay a fee, and then it takes effect immediately. What is notable about this is the fact that you leave the Church by applying to the state for this withdrawal, not to the Church. This shows the hand-in-glove relationship between church and state in Germany.

But this small fee is nominal in comparison to what you save by taking this step. Someone once calculated that an average church taxpayer pays enough church tax over the course of his lifetime to enable him to easily afford a good retirement package, or even a small home, if he were to earn interest on it. This fact is very unique to Germany – that a person automatically pays a separate tax to the Church, along with the taxes that he pays to the state, both collected by the government. However, this applies only to the Catholic and Protestant-Lutheran Churches, which are considered the two mainstream, that is, official, churches in Germany. And regardless of attendance or membership, upon becoming a taxpayer, a person automatically pays this church tax. If this is unacceptable to an individual, that person must go to the respective German government office and request that this money be applied somewhere else.

So if someone wants to become free of these organizations, this is the procedure in Germany. In other countries, there are other ways. If our readers have any questions on this, we will be happy to answer them accordingly and individually.

It is important to realize that if we no longer pay church taxes (in Germany) or church tithes, or if we no longer go to church, we are not dissociating ourselves from the teachings of Jesus, the Christ. Instead, we are dissociating ourselves from an idolatry, a paganism, that the churches embody, even though they have hung the cape "Christ" about their shoulders.

The privileges of the priests –
Cruelly instituted by the powerful

There's another **question** that relates to this: *You mentioned that it is quite possible that elements from the paganism of Babylonia slipped into the Old Testament. Are there grounds for this in the Bible, or what do you base this on?*

Answer: The Israelites were imprisoned in Babylon over several generations. During this time, Cyrus, the King of Persia, conquered Babylon. The history of the return of the Israelites, as allowed by King Cyrus, is found in the Bible. We can read in the book of Ezra how this return was allowed to take place:

In the first year of his reign, King Cyrus issued a decree: Concerning the house of God at Jerusalem, let the house be rebuilt, the place where sacrifices are offered and burnt offerings are brought. (Ezra 6:3)

So their return was linked with the task of rebuilding the temple in Jerusalem. In the same breath, animal sacrifices are mentioned, sacrifices that are described in the Old Testament. However, in another part of the Old Testament it says that the great prophets of the Old Covenant clearly spoke out against these animal sacrifices.

And how did the Israelites react to this order? We can read this in chapter 3:

But many of the priests and Levites and heads of families, old people who had seen the first house on its foundations, wept with a loud voice when they saw this house, though many shouted aloud for joy. (Ezra 3:12)

Here, we can see that opposites are being expressed here: the one shouts for joy, the other weeps. Are they weeping for joy, or perhaps because they feel that something is being brought in or intensified in the rites of the Israelites that have nothing to do with the will of God? And what happened to those who resisted? This question is also quite interesting. From the beginning, with the decree of King Cyrus, we read:

Furthermore I decree that if anyone alters this edict, a beam shall be pulled out of the house of the perpetrator, who then shall be impaled on it. The house shall be made a dunghill. (Ezra 6:11)

And here, quite naturally, a question comes up: If this really were the will of God, that the Israelites go back and rebuild the temple as Cyrus instructed, then why would anyone resist it? And why would anyone have to be threatened with such a horrible punishment? Could it be that through Cyrus' order, those who still knew what the will of God was – that one should not offer up any animal sacrifices – would be cruelly wiped out before their return?

As we continue to read, we find the following:

This Ezra went up from Babylonia. He was a scribe skilled in the law of Moses that the Lord the God of Israel had given; and the king granted him all that he asked, for the hand of the Lord his God was upon him. (Ezra 7:6)

But was this really so? Or did the king grant him everything because Ezra had done what he wanted?

As we continue reading, there is talk about money that Ezra should collect:

With this money, then, you shall with all diligence buy bulls, rams and lambs, and their grain offerings and their drink offerings, and you shall offer them on the altar of the house of your God in Jerusalem. (Ezra 7:17)

And shortly thereafter we read:

We also notify you that it shall not be lawful to impose tribute, custom, or toll on any of the priests, the Levites, the singers, the doorkeepers, the temple servants, or other servants of this house of God. (Ezra 7:24)

So here, the priests are being granted exemption from paying taxes. Surely it is easy to imagine that they themselves slipped this privilege into the Old Testament.

The reformulation of the 5th commandment into "You shall not murder" leaves room to justify killing

And if all this is supposed to have been commanded by God, then what does it have to do with the Ten Commandments, for example, with: *You shall not kill*? Apparently, from the Biblical passages above, it would seem that King Cyrus, the priest Ezra and God were all in agreement, and yet, in God's commandments, He said: "*You shall not kill.*" So is God a God who contradicts himself, or is God the Absolute? Either the commandments of God are false, or these many instructions in the Bible.

Historically, the Church has always taken the right to "correctly" interpret the commandments, and in this particular case, the church interpretation is: The commandment "you shall not kill" is valid only for private persons, but not for the leadership, who may, for example, mete out capital punishment, or give the order to go to war. Apparently, the commandments have been interpreted just as it suits the ecclesiastical leadership.

An attempt to gloss over these contradictions even more is also found in the latest falsification of the Bible where this commandment has been changed from "You shall not kill" to "You shall not murder." When we look at this from a legal point of view, it looks like the following: There is no justification for murder because it is a particularly reprehensible act of killing. But governmental law has also found a lot of justifications for "killing," among other things, particularly where the leadership is concerned. This is probably why the word "kill" was taken out of the commandments of God, so that a justification, when required, could be interpreted into it.

The sacrificial mass –
a crass and mystically elevated practice
of pagan thought in the blood sacrifice

A **question** to the pagan insertions in the Bible that were then taken over by Church Christianity:
In the second program, you explained about paganism's belief in sacrifices. But isn't the celebration of mass in church also a kind of sacrificial mass built around pagan concepts?

Answer: What is being addressed here is the central and worst falsification of the teachings of Jesus of Nazareth. In the so-called "sacrifice of the mass," the Church sees the symbolic re-enactment of the blood sacrifice of Jesus on the cross, but without the blood. At every mass celebrated, the blood sacrifice is again portrayed in theme and symbol. The concept of sacrifice is of ancient pagan origin. Originally, these were human sacrifices, then they became animal sacrifices, and then it again became a human sacrifice, namely, the sacrifice of the Son of God. He is supposed to have come to earth to die as the "sacrificial lamb," so that mankind could be "reconciled with God." This is how it was announced by Paul and adopted by the Church over the centuries. This is why practically every Catholic today believes in this. If someone were to ask, "Why did Jesus come to the earth?" the most frequent answer given is: "to die for us, because only through this could He redeem us."

But Jesus of Nazareth did not come to earth to die; He came to found the Kingdom of Peace, the Kingdom of God, on earth. He came to bring people the "Glad Tidings," the teaching that leads people into a life in the Spirit of God, into peace, into the great unity of life; and above all, it is a teaching that leads people to God in their inner being. We know this from the divine revelations given through Gabriele for today's time. But we also know this, in part, from some passages of the gospels, in particular, from the apocryphal scripts.

This blood sacrifice, this "blood mysticism," so to speak, came into so-called Christianity through Paul. Belief in the idea of sacrifice does not represent the teaching of Jesus, or any Christian teaching, but a Pauline teaching. And this is, by far, the worst falsification of the teachings of Jesus. Because here, it is done as if there were a wrathful God, who is so brutal and cruel, that He requires His own Son as a sacrifice of expiation, and for this reason, sent Him to earth. Can it get any worse or more brutal than that?

"Blood sacrifice" also in war?
Soldiers should sacrifice themselves
for the "Fatherland."
"The canons of war" as the "speaking instruments of the calling grace" of God?

Apropos the concept of "blood sacrifices," in the commandments it says: "*You shall not kill.*" This commandment was rather recently changed to: "*You shall not murder.*" Assuming the Catholic Church and the Lutheran Church are for war, even if it is only a defensive war, then couldn't we look upon the act of shooting people, of killing other people with a weapon, as a human sacrifice that is carried out to rescue or free a state? This would correspond to the claim that "you can kill, but not murder." So, isn't the concept of blood sacrifice also a part of war?

There were certainly many army chaplains who brought this thought to the soldiers in the first and second world wars, in the sense that the soldiers should lay down their life, even sacrifice themselves, for their fatherland. Cardinal Faulhaber, who later was formalized as an alleged resistance fighter against the Third Reich, said as an army chaplain during the first world war: "*The canons of war are the speaking instruments of the calling grace of God.*"[30] This statement carries the thought that war is a process of purification, whereby the moral shortcomings of the people are washed pure in war, and that the soldier should lay down his life and sacrifice himself for this higher goal. The macabre in this lies in the fact that such army chaplains stood on both sides of the front and said the same thing to all the soldiers who then slaughtered each other.

So, blood sacrifice as a thought is actually still a current and relevant thought – but this doesn't make it any less pagan. Because, what did Jesus say as Peter took up the sword?: "*Put your sword back into its place, for all who take the sword will perish by the sword*" (Mt.26:52). This was clearly a warning to us human beings that when we apply violence, this is not in keeping with the spirit of God, but that we will then have to harvest this seed, ourselves.

It is notable that Jesus said this in a so-called defensive situation. Despite the fact that His life was being threatened, He told His disciple to put his sword back. The Church would say: "Hit back. Beat 'em up! You may defend yourself and you may lead a justified war." The whole teaching of a "justified war" is actually exposed as un-Christian through this verse in the Bible, through these very words of Jesus of Nazareth.

But the Church is a bit cunning in this. It doesn't simply say: "We're all for a defensive war," instead, it says: "As a last resort – only when all else fails." The only problem with this is that history teaches us that we have never really used up all other options first – not by a long shot. Instead, it seems the hypocrisy in the Catholic Church simply has no bounds.

The hypocrisy of the Catholic Church takes on extreme forms.
Popes publicly proclaim: A praise to the Inquisition; genocide in the conquest of South America is "a happy guilt," etc.

From this discussion, we can see that facts are clouded and obscured to such an extent, that the hypocrisy of the Church is hardly noticed. But what we are witnessing today can hardly be termed anything but hypocrisy. For example, when the current pope says that he is against embryonic research because he wants "to protect life," and yet, this is the same pope who then sees to it that those he protects in this way are killed in a war that he sanctions, by soldiers who are blessed by his field chaplains.

This hypocrisy of the Catholic Church is also ex- pressed in the fact that the current pope deliberately wants to be connected with Benedict XV, his predecessor by name, who allegedly stood so resolutely for peace in Europe. During the First World War, Benedict XV, head of his church at that time, repeatedly and publicly mourned the disaster of the war that was destroying Europe. However, what did he personally do about it? He saw to it that on both sides – in France and in Germany and in all the states that were engaged in war – the presence of military chaplains was particularly strengthened. Why didn't he simply excommunicate the statesmen who participated in the war?

Meanwhile, Pope Benedict XVI has brought hypocrisy and schizophrenia to new heights. It was he who recently defended the Inquisition. A few weeks before his election to the papacy, he gave a rather brash interview on the ARD German public television program "Contrasts" on March 3, 2005. There he explained: *"We stand in a line of continuity with the Inquisition."* One can hardly believe that he expressed this sentence in as relaxed a manner as he did. But it gets even more incredible, because in the next breath he spoke in the following sense: *"It cannot be denied that the Inquisition brought a certain step of progress to mankind, namely in the sense that those accused were questioned beforehand and given a hearing."*

Isn't this cynicism at its purest form, when we consider the fact that the hearings taking place during the Inquisition were connected with the worst kind of torture, during which so many "questioned" died?

It is an affront to the public when a cardinal, who is a follower of the Inquisition – at that time he was still the leader of the Congregation for the Roman Doctrine of Faith – would so uninhibitedly and openly praise the Inquisition as progress. What kind of reaction would someone get if he were to describe the brutality of a dictator in Chile or even of the Nazis in the Third Reich as progress because in the torture chambers of, in this case, Pinochet or Hitler, people were given a brief hearing before being shot?

"Who Is Sitting on the Chair of Peter?" Such statements as these from the pope give a lot of food for thought …

And this cardinal who more or less supports all this is now the pope, the so-called "Holy Father." This means that as far as the Church is concerned, you can be for killing, for slaughtering – just be sure to serve the Church, and then you are "holy."

This can be seen in numerous examples, including those of the predecessor of the current pope, John Paul II, whom many hope will be canonized. At the time of the 500 year anniversary of the evangelization of South America, he said:

The conquest of Latin America by the Catholic Spanish conquerors may have shown certain violent characteristics, and as such, should be condemned. However, because this truly admir-

*able evangelization contributed to an expansion
in the annals of salvation, in the end, it actually
has become a "happy guilt."*[31]

What kind of cynicism lies behind such an insolent statement of "happy guilt" in face of the many cruelties carried out during the conquest of South America that cost countless lives?

Outgrowths of institutionalized superstitions:
Black Madonnas, host pictures –
"Means of salvation and healing"?
Crawling for indulgences –
Becoming free of sin?

Question:

In an auction on Internet, a Black Madonna from Altötting and a sheet of "host pictures" were offered. What are these?

Answer: Building on this question, we can go right on asking: If a person were to take a small piece of this so-called "host picture" and eat it – does the person now have the possibility to become holy or saintly? And if a person were to buy a so-called "Black Madonna" and gnaw at it daily by shaving off some particles from its body and then ingesting them, can the person come into a blessed or holy state?

But first, what is a Black Madonna? And second, what are these "host pictures" all about?

The custom of the Black Madonna was still around even into the 20th century. Someone may think this custom has to do with the Middle Ages – but no, it apparently is still of interest today, as we can conclude from the question.

We looked this up in the Internet and promptly found an answer: On the website of the Catholic Church in Einsiedeln, Switzerland, we could read the following: "*Small shavings were grated off the Madonna and eaten.*" Or, more exactingly, from a work of reference compiled for Dr. Edmund Müller's collection of relics called "Mittel zum Heil" ("Means of Salvation and Healing,") we can read the following:

A very striking possibility to consume a remedy when in need was to take shavings from the clay figure of a "Black Madonna." Still well known into the 20th century, the Black Madonnas came from Altötting in Bavaria and among the folk, were known as "bodily" copies of grace from Einsiedeln in Switzerland. The latter were held to be miraculous and healing because the clay supposedly had soil and mortar from the Lady Chapel mixed into it as well as relic particles. This held true only for those scraping Black Madonnas that were sold by the convent itself, carrying the seal of authenticity on its back.[32]

One can only hope that with these relic pieces mixed in, no corpses were involved.

In terms of the so-called "host pictures," these were pictures of saints that people actually swallowed. They looked like a sheet of postage stamps, and were swallowed like a communion host.

"Host pictures" could earlier be acquired at many different places of pilgrimage. The buyer assumed that these sheets had been blessed and sanctified by a cleric and if possible, had also been touched by the revered image of grace at the place of purchase.[33]

Back then, there were relics, but also the "relics by touch." As an example, in Bamberg, a nail from the cross of Christ supposedly had been found, that is, it showed up, and then thousands upon thousands of nails were produced which briefly touched that particular nail from the cross. These were then the "relics by touch" and they had, of course, double value. Everything doubled in value if it had come into contact with a relic. This is why the buyers were keen to acquire such relics, including these "host pictures."

In danger or need, the individuals would swallow little pictures the size of postage stamps or give them to their sick cattle. The pictures that were used as sacraments were perceived as a kind of medicine, which bore great powers through priestly blessing.

The book goes on to say that "sacraments" are officially described by the Church as:

> ... *sanctified and blessed objects that promise the believers protection and blessing, keeping them from evil and giving them hope for healing. To these objects belong oil, salt, palm fronds, crosses and pilgrimage medallions ...*

And, of course, the so-called host pictures, as well as the Black Madonnas that were scraped.

> *Still in 1903 the Roman Congregation of Rites permitted the application of host pictures ... The custom of swallowing small pictures has its origin in ancient times.*[34]

So swallowing holy pictures was also a pagan custom.

If any other religious community were to do such a thing, their mental state would come under serious question. And, if anyone were to recommend and offer a Black Madonna in Internet for the purpose of eating particles from it to promote some kind of healing process, surely in any community, the health authorities would have to intervene. There is not only a certain madness to this, but it is even a health hazard.

We received yet another **question** concerning such odd customs:

> *Where does the custom of crawling on one's knees to gain absolution come from – like they do in Altötting or on the steps in Rome?*

Answer: This particular custom certainly is related to doing penance. The people seem to believe that by imposing certain expiatory measures on themselves, by making a certain external effort, which at the same time should cause pain, that somehow, they become free of their sins or of punishment for their sins.

Such practices also existed in paganism. This was done in connection with the so-called confession, which was present in Jainism, in the Cult of Anaetis in the Samothracian Kabira mysteries, or with Isis. We can read the following in a book by Karl-Heinz Deschner entitled "Der gefälschte Glaube":

> ... *where before the threats of the priests, the repentant sinners threw themselves onto the temple floor, rammed the holy portal with their heads, and pleaded to the pure ones with kisses and made pilgrimages ...*

(According to Deschner, the practices just described were in advanced religions):

> ... *while in the primitive religions after an admission of sin, wood splinters and straw were spun in the air and everyone rejoiced, for all sins had been scattered with the wind.*[35]

In some mystery cults, people would admit their guilt before the priest as the representative of divinity, in order to become free again of the consequences. "*In the Isis religion*," writes Deschner, "*where one found remission from apostasy*" – that is, remission from renouncing one's faith – "*there was a com-*

plete practice of indulgences, as later developed in Catholicism." [36]

Doctrinal statements of the Holy See: Absurdities and unbelievable nonsense. Whoever doesn't believe is "excommunicated," damned and condemned

We have already addressed the fact that certain things taught by the Catholic Church have to be believed according to its regulations. If a person doesn't believe in these, then he is eternally damned.

According the book by Neuner and Dupuis, in No. 1005, we read:

The Holy Roman Church firmly believes, professes and preaches that "no one remaining outside the Catholic Church, not only pagans" but also Jews, heretics or schismatics, can become partakers of eternal life; but they will go to the "eternal fire prepared for the devil and his angels," unless before the end of their life they are joined to it ... (No. 1005) [37]

What kind of book is "Neuner-Roos" or Neuner-Dupuis? It would be interesting to read what it says on the inside cover of Neuner-Roos:

This book contains the most important documents about the Catholic belief from the times of the apostolic creed until today. But this is not about going through two thousands years of church history and portraying all the dogmatic strife and decisions, but to take those church teaching documents that have a particularly special meaning for the church design of divine revelation and publish them in a German edition ... Particularly today it is the right and duty of the believer to know what the Church has itself said and is saying in the documents of the doctrines of faith.[38]

Dear reader, perhaps you would like to check this out for yourself? The book by Neuner-Roos is available. It is entitled "The Teaching of the Catholic Church as Contained in Her Documents." This book is truly extraordinarily informative reading material. You will be astounded, and perhaps, through this, you may even be moved to follow the recommendation found in the book of Revelations in the Bible to leave this congregation.

We are not examining these unbelievable oddities and cruelties because there is some kind of institution or clan that prescribes such things for their members or adherents. Anyone can believe what he wants and be happy with it in our state. The reason why we are taking a closer look at all these oddities, these unbelievable, one can say, perversities, is because they have been labeled Christian and are supposed to have something to do with Jesus of Nazareth. As Christians we feel called upon to set the record straight. It is enough that Jesus, the Christ, has been slandered, mocked, ridiculed and abused for 2000 years. It is time to bring an end to this abuse. As Original Christians, we have decided to do this and we ask you, dear reader, to analyze what you read here and ask yourself: Who is actually sitting on the Chair of Peter? Does it really have anything at all to do with Jesus, the Christ? Or isn't the truth rather the opposite of what the one who sits there claims?

Shouldn't the "representative of God,"
at the helm of the globe, be able to
command the elements?
Jesus of Nazareth could

We received the following **question**:
I read that Australians were being called to set aside July 24 as a national day to pray for rain. Three broad Church networks have united to invite Australia's Christians to engage in 40 days of prayer in the face of a severe drought.[39] If I ask God for rain, then doesn't this mean that God is responsible for whether it rains or not? So, where does this conviction come from? Isn't it a pagan belief?

And a further **question**:
Do the Original Christians pray for rain?

Answer: In paganism, in the polytheism of idolatry, it was customary to have several gods responsible for the weather, and especially for rain. With the Teutons it was the God Thor; with the Egyptians it was the God Seth who later became the God Baal; with the Greeks, Zeus was the god of weather, and with the Mesopotamians they were the gods Anu and Enlil, just to name a few.

Back then, people believed the gods were responsible for the weather and because of this, these gods needed to have sacrifices brought to them to positively influence the weather. So if the Catholic Church now calls on everyone to pray to God for rain, this is very much in line with pagan tradition.

In this pagan tradition it was also customary to have certain persons claim to be representatives of the gods. We need only think of the pharaohs in Egypt. But this is also the case in Catholicism, where the pope is seen as the "representative of Christ." In Neuner-Roos we can read the following about the pope: "*The Roman Pontiff has primacy in the whole world*" (No. 349) and in the crowning rites of the pope that reached into the 20th century, as the pope was introduced into his office he was told: "*Know that you are the father of all princes and kings, at the helm of the globe.*"[40]

This statement was last used at the coronation ceremony of Pope Paul IV in 1963. But while the pope was still at the helm of the globe, what did he actually direct? When we look around our world today, we could ask if he was the one at the helm of epidemics, or of the hardships in our world? Or was he at the helm of the natural disasters, the floods that have been experienced? Is he at the helm of all the disasters that befell human beings, nature and the animals?

According to such a logical conclusion this would mean that he is at the helm of the disasters that are visited upon the people. But still today, whether he claims to be at the helm of the globe or not, he is also revered as a "saint." So then he must be able to control the rain, the flood disasters, the illnesses, the earthquakes – or even, for example, the tsunami. He must be able to control the elements; it actually should be rather simple for him to do.

He lets himself be revered and addressed as the "representative of God." But if the effect of his representation should be as just mentioned, there are only two possibilities: Either he only pretends to be the representative of God but has no such power – he cannot even heal his own illnesses – or what happens on earth, actually happens with his participation. But then, he would not be the representative of the God of love, of the Father of all people, and he could only be the representative of the god of the underworld.

So, who is sitting on the Chair of Peter?

In the Bible we can read *"Subdue the earth"* (Gen.1:28). What does this mean? We realize that if the pope is at the helm of the globe, then he must be able to control the earth – the floods and so on.

Jesus commanded the elements. In Matthew there's the story about how the disciples were sitting in a boat on the lake and were afraid of the storm that rose and Jesus called out and *"rebuked the winds and the sea; and there was a dead calm"* (Mt.8:26). So, Jesus could do it, but the "representative of God" cannot.

Perhaps, he can, but only in one direction. This is what we have been examining from many different angles: Destroy everything. We have talked about killing, about abuse, about exploitation, destruction. In face of the past and present deeds of the Holy See, to *"subdue the earth"* must mean, all in all, to destroy the earth. For this is how it has always been done by the Catholic Church and the representatives of this mindset.

Another **question** was included in this letter to us: *Do the Original Christians pray for rain?*

Answer: No, the Original Christians do not pray for rain. We know that God has given us a wonderful planet. Our task is to live in harmony with nature and the world of animals. If this sentence *"subdue the earth"* had been understood correctly, it would still be a beautiful planet today, because the people would have lived in unity with nature and the animal world. But unfortunately, this is not the case. Our environment is being increasingly destroyed and this has led to climatic changes – none of which is God's fault, but our fault. We human beings have caused this destruction, and in part, even willfully.

So when Original Christians pray, then they don't pray that it rain or snow, or that there be good weather. Jesus taught us to pray in such a way that the Will of God can take place, and specifically, this means that we pray, for example, for nature that is suffering so much. However, a prayer can become effective only when we strive to apply it in the deed, and this means that we ask ourselves in this particular case what we can do to help alleviate the suffering of nature, and then do it.

We need neither a Catholic nor a Protestant Church. We need Jesus, the Christ. The mighty Spirit of love dwells in every person

Jesus, the Christ brought us the lowest common denominator. He taught us, for example: *"Do to others as you would have them do to you"* (Mt.7:12). This sentence is generally known as the "Golden Rule." Said in a different way, this means: What you don't want others to do to you, don't do to anyone else, either. If this were kept by all people worldwide, we would no longer need a Catholic Church that practices paganism. We wouldn't need the Lutheran Church either, which is really an appendage of the Catholic Church, anyway.

We need only Jesus, the Christ. And Jesus taught us to go into a quiet room and to talk to God, our Father, there.

Because God is the Spirit of love.

God is the Spirit of peace.

God is the Spirit of unity.

The mighty Spirit of love dwells in every person, for every person is the temple of the eternal Spirit, the spirit of our eternal Father. In the quiet chamber, when we become calm and quiet and pray to within and fulfill our prayers, then step by step we will also live in the commandments of God and in the teachings of Jesus, the Christ. And then we change to the positive, to the good, and the great, mighty spirit of our Father can be active through us.

This is, in general terms, the teaching of the Original Christians.

From Jesus, the Christ, we have heard: *"Do to others as you would have them do to you."* Or, what you don't want others to do to you, don't do to anyone else either – neither person, nor animal, nor plant.

Whoever fulfills the teachings of Jesus, the Christ, lets everything on, in, and over the earth live, because the life is God. Whoever wantonly destroys and kills is acting against the love of God.

The early Christians lived according to the teaching and the example given by Jesus of Nazareth. The disastrous turn of development into a totalitarian cult of idolatry, into the Catholic Church

Following is the fourth part of our series "For the Analytical Mind – Who Is Sitting on the Chair of Peter?"

The early Christians were followers of Jesus, the Christ.
They incorporated His simple teaching into their way of thinking and living

The first Christian communities were formed from the circle of people that Jesus of Nazareth had gathered around Himself. Early communities were formed without priests, without a hierarchy. There was no one among them who set the tone, much less a kind of pope who said what was right; instead, what emerged at the beginning was a loose affiliation of independent communities. The members of these early communities held everything in common. There is even a passage in the New Testament that expresses this. It says:

Now the company of those who believed were of one heart and soul, and no one said that any of the things which he possessed was his own, but they had everything in common. (Acts 4:32)

Even if it is only one sentence, it does express how the early Christians lived. They were equal before the law; they had equal rights – including the women. Everyone lived from the work of his own hands. There were living and working communities. In part, there were also housing communities, which produced what they needed to live, and which always gave something of what they had to the poor.

The important characteristic of the early Christians of that time is the fact that they were followers of Jesus, the Christ, because, in their way of thinking and living, they incorporated the teachings of this great Spirit, who is our Redeemer.

They may not have been perfect, but in their daily lives they worked toward putting into practice the spiritual principles that Jesus of Nazareth had taught. They did not hold a communion ritual, but rather ate together, remembering Jesus of Nazareth, who had brought them this teaching. While partaking of the food, they made themselves aware that the Spirit of God is effective in the food; they respected the life that is in all things. They did not have a ritual of baptism. They simply accepted people into their circle. Everything was far more simple and plain and ingenious than what the churches have made of it.

So how did the early Christians of that time treat Mother Earth, the plants and animals? There are passages in the letters exchanged between the first Christians that substantiate the fact that they ate no meat. It can be said with certainty that the members of the early communities for the most part ate no meat.

For example, we can read a text written by Minucius Felix, an early Christian of that time, in a dialog he had with Octavius where he said: *"... and so much do we shrink from human blood, that we do not use the blood even of eatable animals in our food."*[41]

We know of James, the brother of Jesus and first leader of the first community in Jerusalem, that it was said of him that *"He drank no wine nor strong drink, nor did he eat flesh."*[42] And mentioned several times in the translations, we read, *"he wore no garment made of wool, but one of linen."* This would indicate that he was quite deliberate in respecting the life of animals.

We also find in the apocryphal scriptures – meaning those writings that were not included in the Bible – many passages that clearly show that the apostles were vegetarian. In one, it is said of Peter: *"...that I use only bread and olives, and rarely pot-herbs;"*[43] Or of Matthew: *"Matthew partook of seeds, and nuts, and vegetables, without flesh."*[44] And according to the report by [church father] Epiphanius (Against

Heresy 78:13,4), the apostle John was also a vegetarian.[45]

But even the church fathers bore witness to the fact that early Christians ate no meat. For example, John Chrysostom, born in Antioch circa 347 and generally considered the most prominent Doctor of the Greek Church, said:

> *No streams of blood are amongst them, nor cutting up of flesh, … neither are there unpleasing smells of meat amongst them, … neither runnings and tumults, and disturbances, and wearisome clamors; but bread and water, the latter from a pure fountain, the former from honest labor. But if any time they should be minded to feast more sumptuously, their sumptuousness consists of fruits, and greater is the pleasure there than at royal tables.*[46]

All the early Christians lived from the work of their hands – just as it says in the early Christian regulations of the community:

> *But if one cannot, or will not, work with his hands, then according to your insight, consider how you can achieve that an inactive Christian does not live in your midst. But if he does not want to do this, then he is one who wants to do business with his Christianity. Be aware of such people.*[47]

From this, it is clear that there were no priests in the first communities.

It is also fitting that no hunters and no soldiers were allowed to join the first communities. They had to give up this occupation before they were accepted into the community. It was clear to the early Christians that killing people and animals violates the laws of God, and they kept the law. And so, many occupations do not correspond to the early Christian concept, as we can derive from the regulations of the community:

> The professions and businesses of those who are to be taken into the community have to be examined. Whoever is a sculptor or a painter should be instructed not to paint any pictures of idols; he should stop this or be turned away. Whoever is a charioteer or athletic contestant or a circus fighter or the teacher of these, whoever is an animal fighter, a hunter or an official assistant in fighting games shall stop this or he shall be turned down. If someone is a priest or watchman for idolatry, he should give this up or be rejected. A military official serving as policeman is not allowed to kill. If he is ordered to kill in service, he may not do this. If he does not want to follow these instructions, then he should be turned out. A governor or mayor who is clothed in the dignity of crimson and administers the judicial sword should give this up or he should be rejected.[48]

All this shows that the early Christians took the divine commandments very seriously and kept them.

Charismatic tasks of the early Christians in the communities: Prophets, teachers, healers; they lived what they taught

Since there were no mediators between the people in the early communities and God – no priests and the like – how was the connection between them and the divine world kept up?

There is a passage in the New Testament, in the second letter of Peter, where this is clearly expressed. There it says:

And we have the prophetic word made more sure. You will do well to pay attention to this as to a lamp shining in a dark place, until the day dawns and the morning star rises in your hearts. (2. Pet.1:19)

So the prophetic word was among the first Christians. God spoke to the first Christians through enlightened men and women, and to all those who wanted to hear it, just as God spoke to the Israelites through the great prophets in the Old Covenant. We can also see this in another passage, in Paul's first letter to the Corinthians, where we read the following:

And God has appointed in the church first apostles, second prophets, third teachers, then workers of miracles, then healers, helpers, administrators, speakers in various kinds of tongues. (1 Cor.12:28)

It is clear that there were certain tasks in the first communities: There were, for one, the healers, who did not heal from themselves, but who helped intensify the self-healing forces in a person seeking healing through their prayers. It was a healing given through prayer and faith, ultimately, through the power of God. There were teachers, who passed on what Jesus of Nazareth had said to the people, and there were prophets.

These tasks in the community were not carried out in an authoritarian manner. Instead, they were based on charisma, that is, on the spiritual radiation of the person. The people who carried out these tasks were measured on whether what was taught through them was also expressed in their daily life, in their behavior. When this was not the case, it became clear that they were not suited for their task.

The "administrator" and "overseer,"
who took care more of the external duties,
took over power and became bishops
and priests, thus joining the ranks
of pagan tradition

Then there were the administrators who oversaw the community supplies, those who administered the money and those who carried out the tasks of care-takers or janitors. These administrators were referred to as the "episkopoi," which is Greek for overseer. It is from this that the word "bishop" emerged, and it was the bishops who later took over power. There were also the elders, the "presbyters," from which the name "priest" was derived. Thus, those who had prin-cipally external tasks, later called priests and bish-ops, were the ones who took over, and the other three task areas, the prophets, teachers and healers, whose charismatic tasks were far more important for the life of the community from a spiritual point of view, were suppressed.

So how did the so-called elders suddenly work their way into becoming priests? How was this arranged? *In the year 117 after Christ, a certain Ignatius of Antioch sent letters of instruction to other early Christian communities saying: Let the laity be subject to the deacons; the deacons to the pres-*

*byters; the presbyters to the bishop; the bishop
to Christ, even as He is to the Father.*
And then he also writes:
*My son, honour thou God and the king. And
say I, Honour thou God indeed, as the Author
and Lord of all things, but the bishop as the high-
priest, who bears the image of God – of God,
inasmuch as he is a ruler, and of Christ, in his
capacity of a priest.*[49]

The word "bishop" was not an invention of the early
communities, but was already a term used for the
functions of priests or overseers in pagan cults that
existed in the surrounding areas. In the book by Karl-
heinz Deschner, "Abermals krähte der Hahn," we can
read the following:
*In the writings of Homer, Aeschylus, Sophocles
and Pindar, the bishops were referred to as the
gods, regarded as overseers of the people's
good and bad deeds. Plato and Plutarch also
used the word for educators. Itinerant philosophers from Kynos were also called this. But even
in the second century before Christ, there were
cult officials called bishops. According to the
theologian [C.] Schneider, the Christian term for
bishop differs from pagan analogies only
through the dictatorial power associated with it.*[50]
This means that the bishops who took over in early
Christianity practiced an even stronger dictatorial pow-

er than did the bishops of pagan cults. They made a connection with this pagan root and created such an unparalleled ruling power, that one can only rightly speak of a totalitarian cult of idolatry.

The early Christian communities lived in an environment of idolatry, elements of which infiltrated early Christianity more and more

Priests and bishops were also in the pagan cults, even popes. The word "papa," for example, is a derivative of Pater Patrum, the "father of fathers." He was the highest pope in the Mithras cult, and the whole hierarchy, as it is known in the Catholic Church today, stemmed from these cults of idolatry.

Anyone who reads about early Christian history in the first years after Jesus of Nazareth quickly realizes that cults existed in the whole surrounding area, not only the traditional Jewish cult, but also the cult of Mithras, whose adherents practiced the cult of the graves. There, all consecrations took place on burial grounds, similar to what is done in the Catholic faith today when the follower of Peter allegedly receives his office from the grave of Peter. The Mithras cult not only practiced the cult of the dead, but also sacrificed animals.

All this marked the environment surrounding early Christianity. It would seem that these and other practices from this environment were gradually introduced into early Christianity. But none of it came from Jesus.

The strongly determining influence of Paul contributed very decisively to the almost total dissociation of early Christianity from its origin, from the teachings of Jesus of Nazareth

Paul played an important role in this, for he was markedly influenced by a Roman polytheism that developed from paganism, and moreover, had never even lived with Jesus of Nazareth. Paul, who never came to know early Christianity firsthand, brought his ideas into early Christianity in a very dominating way. These were, on the one hand, an authoritarian way of thinking, and on another, he put women in second place, which was not the case at all in early Christianity, where many women were active in the capacity of prophets. And among those who followed Jesus of Nazareth, accompanying him on his journeys, there were always many women. But it wasn't only these two aspects – Paul took a great deal away from early Christianity, bringing his pagan ideas in its stead.

Paul probably brought much more of his pagan ideas into the gospels than is generally thought. In his second letter to Timothy, we can read, for example:

Do your best to come to me soon ... Luke alone is with me. Get Mark and bring him with you; for he is very useful in serving me ... When you come bring ... the books, and above all the parchments. (2 Tim.4:9-11)

This means that Paul was in close contact with Mark, to whom is ascribed the writings of the Gospel of Mark, and with Luke, who is believed to have written the Gospel of Luke.

A second source tells us even more. The Muratorian Fragment, an ancient Latin document presently located in the Abrosian Library of Milan, Italy, was discovered and first printed by Lodovico Antonio Muratori in the 18th century. It is part of a book transcribed 1000 years earlier, and the words from the fragment are generally considered to be part of a document from as early as the second century, making it one of the oldest documents available. It says there that Paul had with him a legal expert – according to another translation, a scholar. He was a physician named Luke. And it reads:

Luke, the well-known physician, after the ascension of Christ, when Paul had taken with him as one zealous for the law, composed it in his own name, according to [the general] belief. Yet he himself had not seen the Lord in the flesh.[51]

So neither Luke nor Paul ever experienced Jesus during His time on earth, yet they wrote a gospel, and as it says here, apparently together. So it is quite possible that Paul exerted a much greater influence on the writings of the gospels than is generally assumed.

So how did Paul come to have such authority in early Christianity?

The man Paul felt a certain admiration for the early Christianity he had come to know, but he also had many authoritarian ideas. And in many respects, Paul did not do things as Jesus had taught, for example, in His words: *"For whoever wants to be first must be last of all and servant of all"* (Mk.9:35). Paul, who did not have the living example of Jesus of Nazareth before his eyes, had a certain drive for power. In one of his letters to the Galatians, for instance, he wrote: *"But even if we, or an angel from heaven, should preach to you a gospel contrary to that which we preached to you, let him be accursed"* (Gal.1:8). From these words it becomes clear that in his world of thoughts some ideas were quite threatening to those of different mind. His body of thought was closely linked with the ideas and cults from the pagan surroundings. It was in this way that very gradually something emerged that no longer had anything in common with the true early Christianity. Imperiousness and a hierarchy of officials joined together, and a church gradually evolved from early Christianity.

It is said that Paul had a vision and that he received the words of the Lord when Christ appeared to him and said: "*I Am Jesus, whom you are persecuting*" (Acts 9:5). According to the story of Paul that has been passed down through the ages, it was at this point that he stopped persecuting this Jesus and joined His ranks.

But even if Paul stopped persecuting Jesus, this still did not mean that he gave up his claim to office, or that he had studied the teachings of Jesus and accepted the teachings of the Lord for himself. Paul went into early Christianity claiming that he had heard the Lord, and this alone gave him the authority to now implement things as he conceived them; soon after, he brought in regulations.

Jesus of Nazareth, for instance, expressly rejected concepts of sacrifice in the sense of having a slaughter victim – something which we have already determined. Yet Paul took this concept from paganism and introduced it into early Christianity. He is also the author of the concept that Jesus of Nazareth had to be sacrificed in so bloody a manner, in order to reconcile God with mankind – a concept that was fully foreign to Jesus of Nazareth, but which, however, Paul introduced.

With this, he basically makes the connection to the blood cults we have already heard about. The well-known historian Karlheinz Deschner also writes about this in his book, "Abermals krähte der Hahn":

Again and again, Paul preaches about reconcili-
ation and redemption, about the means of
atonement "in His blood," of redemption "through
His blood" of peacemaking, "through His blood
that was shed on the cross." [52]

But the second and perhaps even worse falsification of the teachings of Jesus of Nazareth took place
through Paul when he spoke in the following sense:
What is decisive is that you believe in God and in
Christ, His Son; the deeds in the following of the
Nazarene are not so decisive. Paul taught: "*For we
hold that a person is justified by faith apart from works
prescribed by the law*" (Rom.3:28).

This is quite in opposition to the many statements
about James, who was called "a servant of God and
of the Lord Jesus Christ," and who belonged to the
core group of the early community in Jerusalem. He
said: "*What good is it, my brothers and sisters, if you
say you have faith but do not have works? Can faith
save you?*" And he also said: "*So faith by itself, if it
has no works, is dead.*" Or the following: "*Do you want
to be shown, you senseless person, that faith apart
from works is barren?*" And lastly: "*You see that a
person is justified by works and not by faith alone.*"
(Jas.2:14,17,20,24).

And what did Jesus say? The following is quoted
from the Bible:

Everyone then who hears these words of mine and does them will be like a wise man who built his house on the rock. And the rain fell, and the floods came, and the winds blew and beat on that house, but it did not fall, because it had been founded on the rock. And everyone who hears these words of mine and does not do them will be like a foolish man who built his house on the sand. And the rain fell, and the floods came, and the winds blew and beat against that house, and it fell, and great was the fall of it. (Mt.7:24-27)

Paul falsified the teachings of Jesus in still many other points: He totally adapted Christianity to the concepts of the Roman Empire, by declaring that a Christian must obey the authority of this world, because it is instituted and instructed by God and does not bear the sword in vain; it is the servant of God to execute his wrath on the wrongdoer. (Rom.13:1-4) A teaching that, when we look back, had a devastating effect over the subsequent 2000 years. And yet, Jesus said: *"Render to Caesar the things that are Caesar's and to God the things that are God's"* (Mt.22:21). Or in another place even: *"We must obey God rather than men"* (Acts 5:29).

Of course, the Church has been glad to seize upon the words of Paul, because they justify the death penalty or even war, for which it has often blessed weapons.

On another issue, which is not insignificant, Paul apparently had a big problem with vegetarianism, because the following sentence comes from him: "*Eat whatever is sold in the meat market without raising any question on the ground of conscience*" (1 Cor. 10:25). Of course, this has had devastating consequences right up until today. Billions of animals have been slaughtered because of this sentence in the Bible. But we know and have already heard that the first Christians lived as vegetarians. This statement from Paul stands in crass opposition to what Jesus taught, and also to what the early Christians sincerely endeavored to live.

Early Christianity was broken apart through slander purposefully spread by the caste of priests, using incitement, persecution, torture and murder

And so, Paul spoke against Jesus. Jesus' body of thought was still alive in the early Christians of that time. They wanted to honor Jesus by fulfilling His teachings step by step. So how was it that Paul, with his superstitions, his polytheism, his authoritarian way of thinking, was able to gain a foothold in the first communities?

On the one hand, Paul founded many new communities, which had little contact with the early Christian communities in Jerusalem and in Palestine. For this reason, he was probably able to spread his ideas there quite unchallenged. On the other hand, however, there were also many external factors that weakened early Christianity. Right from the beginning, defamatory statements were spread against the early Christians. It was said that the early Christians killed children or practiced some sort of sexual orgies and the like. Rumors were purposefully spread against them and they were often used as scapegoats. In time, the Roman emperors began to act on these rumors and to persecute the Christians. The result was that the best people in the early communities were the first to fall victim to these persecutions; they were the most steadfast and clearest believers. After such persecutions, people from outside joined the early Christians, bringing their own ideas, which they had taken with them from their pagan rituals. With such pressures from without as well as from within, early Christianity was quite successfully weakened over the course of time.

But it would be interesting to ask: Who spread such rumors? Who initiated the persecution of the early Christians?

From the New Testament it is clear that Jesus of Nazareth was being slandered and accused by the caste of priests of that time. They were saying such things as "that is a son of the devil," and "he teaches about a false God." They called Him a sectarian, and the people who followed Him were called the "sect of the Nazarenes." We know this term from the Acts of the Apostles (Acts 24:5). Later in the Roman Empire, it was again the priests who spread such defamations, hand in hand with governmental authorities. The persecution against the first true Christians was carried out by the imperial administration. It was in alliance with the gossipmongers and calumniators among the caste of priests, so that even then, state and priesthood worked hand in hand against the early Christians.

From early Christian writings during the years 50 to 130 AD, there is even something passed down about this. It comes from St. Justin Martyr, who accused the priests in Jerusalem, writing:

… you selected and sent out from Jerusalem chosen men through all the land to tell that the godless heresy of the Christians had sprung up, and to publish those things which all they who knew us not speak against us.[53]

"Who knew us not." This means that foreigners went into the cities and to the authorities, the Roman ruler, for instance, saying: "A sect is in your city; you should watch them." So priests sent agents out to wherever such early communities developed, so that they could slander them, saying: "Watch out, that is a sect." Roman law, written on 12 bronze tablets, stated that no new god could be introduced except one approved by the emperor. At that time, the Christian God had not yet been accepted by the emperor, so anyone who stated before the court: "I am Christian," was destined to die. These men, hired calumniators, managed to bring things to such a point that, above all, the strong, carrying members of the communities were arrested and then martyred and killed.

When we read the letter from St. Justin Martyr, it sounds quite familiar: Apparently, already then, there were agents of character assassination, today we would call them "sect-watch agents." Such a function has been kept up until today, and has thus been around for about 1900 years.

Early Christianity was turned into its opposite through the dictatorial and totalitarian power-wielding practices of the bishops

Early Christianity was broken through gossip, incitement, persecution and certainly through murder and the like, as well. So how is it that the bishops were able to push themselves to the forefront? How did it come to develop into an institution?

The bishops held the longest whip in hand. They managed the money of the community, and of course, gave money only to those who served them. Through this, they were able to expand their position of power. They also strove to take as many new members as possible into the communities. New members meant more income, and more income generated more power. But to take in more members, they had to make compromises on the teachings over and over again. And so, they complied with the spirit of those times, the pagan mystery cults, by seeing to it that the faith being taught in the early communities back then accommodated, for the most part, the indolence of the people. A part of this was a God who forgives all sins – solely by believing. This concept characterized ancient idolatry. It was taken up by Paul and later we find it again in a very pronounced way with Luther.

When the Christians were persecuted, the bishops afterward gave orders to take into the communities as quickly as possible all those who had fallen away from early Christianity by bringing sacrifices to the emperor. Thus, the bishops watered the whole thing down every which way; their striving in every respect was to see that the communities adapted to the authority of the Roman state. One can see this, for instance, by the fact that women were forbidden to have leading functions, just as a woman was not allowed to have a leading position in the Roman state. In the first communities, however, women had often been at the head of the living communities. So in this, too, the bishops turned early Christianity into its opposite.

The wealthiest early community was in Rome. This is very clearly reflected in the letters from early Christianity. When the communities met, their most important function was to help the needy, the poor. It is very moving to read about. The early Christians had to know very exactly such things as: Who lives where? Who is poor or who is a widow? They really had to know the various parts of the city in order to help those who needed it.

The early Christians literally worked to support and carry the poor. The community of Rome alone cared daily for 1500 people in need. The early Christians in Rome also cared for the poor communities like Jerusalem or those in Asia Minor that weren't as well off. In this way, Rome gained a certain status, because there were more rich citizens in its community. In time, they became arrogant. In the year 190, the Roman bishop – he was already calling himself "bishop" then – denounced all the communities that did not want to accept the Roman Easter customs. These were pagan customs, and although the early Christians in Asia Minor didn't pay much attention to this, it was clear that the stage was being set for further developments. Rome had begun to pull the strings and to make ultimatums, introducing elements that Jesus never spoke about.

It still took several centuries before Rome really became the ruling power – at least in the western regions of the Church. Until today, in the Eastern Orthodox Church, Rome is not the religious capital. But in earliest times, Rome's claim to being "first" had already started.

At a later date, Bishop Victor I excommunicated all the churches in Asia Minor. This process, whereby pagan priests and idolaters gained ground with their ideas and rituals, began already in the second century after Christ. Already at that time, they started to introduce sacraments. They had altars; after some time the bishop sat on a separate chair, which eventually became a throne.

During the 3rd century, the priests started wearing their own special garments. This came relatively late in the century. They had processions and pilgrimages just like the pagan cults. They began to revere saints. Jesus may have expressed the beatitudes, but He never said that a person should be beatified – this is something totally different. And saints never had a place in the teachings of Jesus, the Christ. For what reason? Every person had – and has! – the possibility to find his own way to God in himself. So why would he need "saints," who are supposed to be the mediators in heaven? Church holidays were introduced that were celebrated on the same days as pagan holidays. Until today, many important church holidays are pagan holidays. Christmas, for instance, was the celebration of the highest sun god: Sol invictus, the never vanquished sun. Mary's Assumption on the 15th of August was an important celebration of Diana, the great pagan "mother-goddess."

So this process, starting very early and then continuing over the course of about 200 years, led to the fact that the original teaching of Jesus of Nazareth, that is, the early Christian teaching, actually turned into a pagan religion. When Emperor Constantine (285-337) then made his appearance, he "finished it off," naming early Christianity the state religion, once and for all.

And the Church, which had already become largely pagan, fell for this hook, line and sinker. We can see this in its relationship to war and violence. In the book "Abermals krähte der Hahn," by Karlheinz Deschner, we read for instance:

In the year 313, Constantine guaranteed total freedom of religion to the Christians. In 314 the Synod of Adelate concluded that soldiers who had deserted should be excommunicated. Anyone who threw down his weapons was excommunicated; before that, those who did not throw down their weapons had been excommunicated.[54]

Emperor Constantine made what had become a thoroughly pagan church into a state church

During the time of Emperor Constantine, there were two equally strong religions: Christianity and the Mithras cult. The latter had 800 churches in Rome. Today, when going through these churches, they all have a central aisle, the benches left and right, an altar up front, steps going up, an arch up above and a basin of consecrated water at the entrance – they all look just like a simple Catholic Church.

The roots of Catholicism in the Mithras cult are very clear to see. One could almost say that the Catholic Church actually developed less from early Christianity than from pagan cults. At most, it took the name and the gospels from Christianity. The Mithras cult also had seven sacraments and even the word "sacrament" was used in this cult.

The Mithras cult was one of many pagan cults practiced at the time of the Roman Empire. And it was most probably introduced to Rome by Roman soldiers returning from Babylonia.

In a book by Johannes Leipoldt, "Umwelt des Urchristentums," we can read the following:

Mithras is an ancient Iranian god of heaven and light, who was praised in the Avesta, the sacred text of Zoroastrianism, as the guardian of the covenant and the embodiment of those true

*to the covenant. Since about 400 before Christ,
he appears on all inscriptions of royal dynas-
ties.*[55]

It was an ancient teaching of the heavens, a teaching of a god of light, which taught that redemption
goes out from this god of light. This belief in Mithras
started in Babylon and had all sorts of astrological
elements and influences from other cults as well. Influential magicians were its most zealous mission-
aries. A closer look at these magicians, their robes
and how they sit on their throne, shows that it is just
like the pope sitting on the throne today, or the bishops and cardinals. They also had various levels of
priests, just as we know from Catholicism today.

From this same book, "Umwelt des Urchristentums," we see that there were many scriptures available, but it is an indisputable fact that for every rank
there was a special costume or symbol, the transfer
of which was carried out in celebration. Every spiritual office was indelibly connected with insignia, garments and symbols. We also know that in the Mithras
cult the sacrament of baptism was celebrated, as well
as communion, confirmation and a sacrament of
atonement. This may sound quite familiar, but Jesus
never instituted such things, nor did He or the early
Christians want them. The Mithras cult celebrated a
communion as well, not as the early Christians, but
as a ritual, just like it is celebrated today in the Catho-

lic Church. The priests were also active in this ritualistic communion.

In addition, the priest spoke the so-called words of blessing, and he also said (quoting from the above-mentioned book): *"You have saved the men through the shedding of eternal blood."* [56] The blood of the bull, the ritualistic meal, thus promised the initiated a heavenly existence and resurrection. Here, too, we encounter the sacrifice of animals in the pagan cult of priests. The blood sacrifice, which the Catholic Church adopted, had its origin in the Mithras cult, in which they also believed in the resurrection of the flesh. Jesus never said anything about this, but it is taught today in the Catholic Church. The Mithras cult also knew the Day of Judgment and a lot of other components of the Catholic Church regulations. When we read about it and look at the pictures, what we basically see is pure Catholicism.

Several authors have written that Constantine wanted to avoid the discord that two parallel religions would have brought. For this reason, he decided for Christianity. Many officials and soldiers had imported the pagan Mithras cult into Rome and from there carried it into all countries. The soldiers and officials are, of course, the basis for an empire. On the other hand, Christianity had spread equally among the rich as well as the poor. Both religions were on a par with each other and many researchers say that Constantine simply wanted one religion. He wanted peace in his realm, and somehow closed the door on one, thus bringing about a religious unity, or, rather, a religious mishmash in one. At the Council of Nicaea in 325, he forbade the practice of the Mithras cult. Only one religion was allowed to exist in his empire.

The council of Nicaea in 325 was decisive for the introduction of this unified religion as Emperor Constantine intended. At that time, although early Christianity had pretty much changed into its opposite by then, there still existed a current that tried to connect back to original Christianity. These were the so-called Arian Christians, who based themselves on Origen, a great philosopher and thinker who lived in the 3rd century. During his life he fought against the falsification of early Christianity and against the falsification of the Bible. He recognized that something had become seriously wrong and that early Christianity was actually quite different from what it had become. During the persecution of the Christians by Emperor Decius in the year 250, Origen was badly tortured and died of his injuries 4 years later. But his teaching, his body of thought, continued to spread. One of his followers was, for instance, Arius of Alexandria in Egypt, who disseminated his teachings. He was a contemporary of Constantine, and at the Council of Nicaea in 325, the decision was made by the emperor: Not Arius and his teaching were right, but the Church, as he had encountered it in Rome.

Before going any further into these theological differences, it would be interesting to mention that vegetarianism was often a political issue at these councils and synods. For example, we can read from the year 314 that a decree was written and concluded at the Church Synod of Ancyra, that all priests or deacons who were vegetarians should be excommunicated. Literally, we read:

It is decreed that among the clergy, presbyters and deacons who abstain from flesh shall taste of it ... But if they disdain it, and will not even eat herbs served with flesh, but disobey the canon, let them be removed from their order.[57]

"Disobey the canon" implies that eating meat was a rule for anyone, even an important rule for being considered for the priesthood in Catholicism. This is all the more astonishing, considering the fact that all of early Christianity had been vegetarian. And to guarantee that all future members of the Catholic Church actually eat meat, new members had to speak out a curse, a curse against the Nazarenes. It sounds incredible, but this citation is substantiated. New members had to speak the following words: "*I curse the Nazarenes, the stubborn ones, who deny that the law of sacrifice was given by Moses, and who refrain from eating living creatures, never offering sacrifices.*"[58]

It becomes rather clear that still enormous spiritual battles were taking place in the 4th century, a struggle about what the teachings of Jesus of Nazareth really were; and the falsification of these teachings was already very, very far advanced. This was demonstrated at this council by the theological matters of dispute that were up for debate there.

One of these was on the question of whether Jesus of Nazareth is the Son of God or whether he is God himself. Athanasius, Bishop of Alexandria and Confessor and Doctor of the Church, defended the homoousian formula that states that Christ is of the same substance as the Father.[59] For a Roman like Constantine this was familiar territory because the Romans only knew one principle god – Jupiter – and at most, perhaps an incarnation of a god. This is why, in the interest of the unification of his state religion, Constantine decided for the belief that Jesus of Nazareth, that is, Christ, is "the true God from true God,"[60] just as it can be read today in the Nicene Creed. Arius, on the other hand, represented the view of the early Christians, that Jesus of Nazareth is the Son of God, who is filled by God, but not identical with God. This became an important change of course introduced by a Roman emperor.

Today's Original Christians know through the word of God, the prophetic word for our time, that Jesus of Nazareth came to this earth as the Son of God in order to bring the Kingdom of Peace, and that He was filled by the Spirit of His Father – by God.

Arian Christianity continued to exist for several centuries. But the faith of the Roman Catholic Church is still influenced today by the conclusion of the council decreed by Constantine, where it said, that Christ is "of the same substance of the Father, the true God from true God."

It may seem like theological sophistry to argue about who Jesus really was. But the real issue here is the fact that the Church wanted to make its faith as simple as possible. Seen from the point of view of the spirit of the times back then, there was a tendency in the pagan cults to have only one god, a god who absolves all sins if a person performs all rituals in the right way. By then, polytheism had lost some ground. So Christianity should have only one God. To this end, one God was created who was portrayed in three people: God-Father, God-Son, and the Holy Ghost. But the belief of the first Christians was different: There is only one God and Christ, the Son of God, incarnated in Jesus of Nazareth, who brought the people the divine laws of life, and the supporting and guiding spark of Redemption, the Redeemer-power. Because of this, every person has the possibility to experience Christ in himself and to find his way to God through these divine laws, and not through external rituals. That is quite a difference.

Jesus was filled by God and was not God, Himself. He was the Son of God, whom the Father sent, and who was filled by the Spirit of the Father. This vitalized the early Christianity of that time, and vitalizes today's Original Christianity. In all clarity, a mystery cult is a pagan cult. Constantine was shaped by the pagan cults. And ultimately, the actions of the caste of priests of today are an inheritance from Constantine's pagan cult, which was added to the belief in the one God.

This is how it all ended up. Whatever did not come from the Mithras cult came from the cults of Athis, of Dionysus, Hercules, Osiris or Isis. There were many cults that moved in a similar direction; and Constantine himself had lived in this type of cult thinking and therefore supported it. Although he made Christianity the state religion in name, he actually brought these pagan cults into it. Constantine himself was pagan; he still consulted oracles and still had himself printed on coins as a sun god. It was also the custom of that time for the emperor to have himself called a god and people also had to make sacrifices to him as a god. Constantine also was not baptized during his lifetime; it was only at his deathbed that he let himself be given the sacrament of baptism, not by a Roman Catholic priest, but by an Arian Christian. But none of this is of relevance to the Church. Until today, it continues to revere him. Constantine was a cruel person, a person who waged wars, who had his captive opponents thrown to the bears and had his own family killed. But none of this matters to the Holy See! Instead, it reveres Constantine as if he were a saint, because he made the Church into a state religion, and that is what counts for the Church.

Constantine also gave the Church enormous privileges. He had pagan temples dispossessed and turned over to the Church. He freed the clergy of most taxes. He secured the income of the clergy. He gave them huge presents. And right up until today in Germany, the Church is extensively supported by the state. The salaries of bishops and cardinals are paid by the state, to the tune of 8-10,000 Euros per month! The education of theologians, the religion classes in public schools, all this is paid by the state. The churches are also exempted from many, many taxes. When we add all this together, we come to the enormous sum of 14 billion Euros annually in subsidies to the churches by the German state. And this is what the Church loves.

We still have a state church today...

We still have a state church today that is more like a church for government leaders. For who is it that makes pilgrimages to the Holy See? It is the government leaders, who may shake the hand of the head of the Catholic Church, the hand of the one who represents the Chair of Peter.

Over the course of time, the Holy See introduced other laws that are just as terrible as those from the pagan cults – laws that are absolutely contrary to the teachings of Jesus, the Christ.

Perhaps it would be interesting to take a closer look at all the dogmas, rites and cults of today's state, that is, ruling, religion, to find out where the cults came from, where the dogmas and rites came from. In this way everyone can recognize whom he is serving: a Constantinian state religion or Jesus, the Christ?

The cult of Mary and revering relics: Whoever does not believe in this is eternally damned by the Catholic Church. Is a dictatorship trying to rule over a democracy?

During our last program we showed how early Christianity emerged and changed over the course of centuries – from the peaceful teaching of Jesus of Nazareth to an aggressive pagan cult religion called Catholic. It became clear how ever more Roman concepts and other pagan ideas were put into practice against the Christian teaching – sometimes even violently. Today, we will portray in detail how the Holy See almost exclusively bases itself on this pagan foundation. We will shine a light on Catholic tradition, its customs, rites, cults, dogmas, insignia, holidays, etc.

As we go through the details, it will become increasingly difficult to conceive as possible the extent of such a conglomeration of pagan cult concepts.

The Catholic cult of Mary as the "mother of God" is deeply rooted in pre-Christian paganism

The teaching and structure of the Catholic Church in almost all aspects is derived directly from pagan idolatry.

Given this statement, its connection to the cult of Mary becomes clear as an essential component of the Catholic faith. It is the cult of the "mother of God" who, according to a dogma proclaimed by Pius XII, presumably was taken physically up to heaven. Jesus of Nazareth did not speak of His mother as the "mother of God." She was Mary, a simple, modest and devout woman, a woman of the people. So it would be quite interesting to look into how such an odd development took place and above all, what antecedents did this cult have? Looking back, we realize that the cult of a mother of God is deeply rooted in pre-Christian paganism.

For example, it is known that the Egyptian goddess Isis and the Greek goddess Artemis were revered in a similar way as Mary is venerated until today in the Catholic Church. In part, they were even referred to using the same terms as "Queen of the Heavens" or "Star of the Sea" – perhaps some of us know that song "Star of the Sea, I Greet You" that is still sung today in places of pilgrimage honoring Mary. Did Jesus of Nazareth ever refer to Mary, His mother, as "Star of the Sea?" This was the title of the great mother-goddesses in Greece and Egypt. And what is also significant is that the dogma that claims Mary as the mother of God – that is, not only the mother of Jesus, but the mother of God – was decided at the Council of Ephesus in 431, when it declared that the second letter of Cyril to Nestorius was in agreement with the Council of Nicaea.[61] Interestingly enough, Ephesus was the center of the Diana cult, that is, a city where the mother-goddess Diana was particularly revered. Clearly, this is a pagan thought that found its way into the Church.

Perhaps it is interesting to note that Diana was the goddess of the hunt, and at the same time, the "mother of God."

And so, the mother of Jesus became a cult object, a pagan cult object. This went so far that in Altötting, for instance – a place of pilgrimage in Bavaria – so-called "Black Madonnas" were sold right into the 20th century. From a work of reference compiled on Dr. Edmund Müller's collection of relics called "Mittel zum Heil," we can read the following:

A very striking possibility to consume a remedy when in need was to take shavings from the clay figure of a "Black Madonna." Still well-known into the 20th century, the Black Madonnas came from Altötting in Bavaria and were known among the folk as "bodily" copies of grace from Einsiedeln in Switzerland. The latter were held to be miraculous and healing because the clay supposedly had soil and mortar from the Lady Chapel mixed into it as well as relic particles. This held true only for those Madonnas that were sold by the convent itself ...[62]

So relic particles, perhaps even corpse pieces, were added to these Madonnas. Whoever acquired these "religious remedies" scraped some from the clay figure and added it to their food. The monastery itself sold these right into the 20th century. This is just one example to show how far a cult, a pagan cult, will go. But most Catholics don't even know this. Surely this doesn't have the least bit in common with religion, much less with a Christian religion or the teachings of the Nazarene.

Many a church leader may perhaps excuse this as having to do with folklore, or even superstition, but the fact remains that the basic celebrations of this Mary cult are part of church dogma, even to portraying Mary as the "mother of God." She is revered in the Catholic Church as the Madonna with a corona of stars on a crescent moon. This portrait is similar to the Egyptian goddess Isis, who was depicted in exactly the same way.

So Mary was adopted by the Roman Catholic Church, elevated to the mother of God and is portrayed as the direct successor of Egyptian goddesses, such as Isis and other figures of pagan mystery cults. She is the successor of Diana or Artemis, or even Astarte, who was the Phoenician divinity of fertility. And this dogma of enthroning Mary as a mysterious cult goddess developed in Ephesus, a city where the cult of the mother of God had been a custom for centuries. What is also significant is the fact that while the council of Ephesus was trying to eliminate devotion to Diana, the bishops were besieged by crowds demanding: "Give us our Diana of the Ephesians!"[63]

From this, we can deduce that Mary, the woman and mother, is above all women and mothers. If we now think of the fact that particularly Catholic priests are not allowed to marry, could this have something to do with the fact that they might, for instance, marry a simple woman? Instead, they have to "marry," so to speak, the woman of all women and the mother of all mothers.

Similar to this picture of Mary, the Egyptian goddess Isis was often protrayed standing on a half-moon with a crown of stars

Isis and Horus

Semiramis with Tammuz

Indrani with child

Devaki with Krischna

In fact, this is an explanation for the deepest psychological root of celibacy in the Church. The "great mother" was a figure that prevailed in the subconscious of mankind millennia before the emergence of Christianity. Back then, priests of the "great mother" were not allowed to marry; they wore feminine robes and saw themselves as the sons of this great mother. In view of this, the priests, who may not marry a woman, are basically in service to this "great mother," an archetypal figure of pagan origin.

But an important question would be: Why did the Church need to take over this pagan cult of the mother goddess? Could it have something to do with the fact that the Church had portrayed God as a cruel, arbitrary, punishing God, who allegedly can send His children into eternal damnation? So to balance things out, it took the "mother of God," who is a more comforting figure, so that the people would not be left in fear of a "punishing" God.

Mary, the virgin and undefiled woman
who bore God – Whoever doesn't
believe this is eternally damned.
Many who pay their church taxes
or tithes are not aware of this

Now, some may ask, what about the person who doesn't believe in this Mary cult or revere the so-called "mother of God," but simply respects and cherishes her as the mother of Jesus, the physical mother of Jesus? According to church doctrine is this person eternally damned?

The answer is, yes. In the book "The Teaching of the Catholic Church as Contained in Her Documents" by Neuner-Roos, it says:

If anyone does not truly and rightly confess with the Fathers that the holy, ever virginal and immaculate Mary is Mother of God, since in recent days she really and truly conceived, without seed, by the Holy Ghost, the same divine Word who was born before all time and gave birth to him in chastity, her virginity remaining unimpaired after the birth – condemnatus sit. (No. 269)

This would mean that all those who call themselves Protestant are eternally damned, or condemned. So, why do they curry favor with the Holy See?

This is a question that always comes up when there is talk about ecumenism, or when the Protestants make a pilgrimage to the Holy See or gather with it in other ways, and then, as recently happened, a high-ranking cardinal like the cardinal of Cologne, Cardinal Meisner, expresses himself with great reticence on the subject. In the Protestant Press Service release from June 5, 2005, it is reported:

An ecumenical progress is expected by the archbishop of Cologne only between the Roman-Catholic and Orthodox Churches, but not between Catholics and Protestants. With the Reformed Church it is a long and laborious way, said Meisner. We should not fool ourselves with things that cannot be kept.

Sometimes, one could wonder at the spiritual perspicacity of those Protestants who are drawn to the Catholic Church.

Whoever does not pay deep respect
and honor to the relics of the saints
is damned by the Catholic Church.
A cult of the dead: Belief and practice
in this church is based on bones

Being eternally damned by the Catholic Church can happen very quickly. As children, many are compelled to go to church, and in many churches there is a skeleton dressed in beautiful clothing in a glass casket near the altar. What a ghoulish sight for chil-

Skeleton (relic) in St. Peter's Church in Munich

dren! And yet, when a Catholic doesn't believe salvation comes from these skeletons, he is damned.

The Council of Trent decreed the veneration of the corpses of martyrs and damned those who do not believe in relics. We read:

Also, that the holy bodies of holy martyrs ... are to be venerated by the faithful; through which (bodies) many benefits are bestowed by God on men; so that they who affirm that veneration and honour are not due to the relics of saints ... are wholly to be condemned as the Church has already long since condemned, and now also condemns them.[64]

This explanation may not be directly classified as a dogma, but it nevertheless remains an obligation for Catholics to believe this, although it really is deepest paganism.

In ancient Egypt there were many cult sites where the remains of so-called "gods" were venerated, and from which a magical effect was said to emanate. When we read about the relics and the "Black Madonnas," we can see the direct path that leads to the "magic" that still prevails today in the Roman Catholic Church and that has nothing to do with Christianity.

Furthermore, it cannot be excused as mere folklore. This matter of relics was taken in hand by the popes right from the very beginning. We read, for example, the following:

In about 750, long lines of wagons constantly came to Rome bringing immense quantities of skulls and skeletons which were sorted, labeled and sold by the popes. Graves were plundered by night and tombs in churches were watched by armed men.[65]

Gregorovius wrote: "Rome was like a moldering cemetery...."[66] In the church of St. Prassede there is a marble tablet still today, on which is written that in the year 817 Pope Pascal had the bodies of 2300 martyrs brought from cemeteries into this church. And when Pope Bonifatius VI transformed the Pantheon into a Christian church in the year 609, *"twenty-eight cartloads of sacred bones were said to have been*

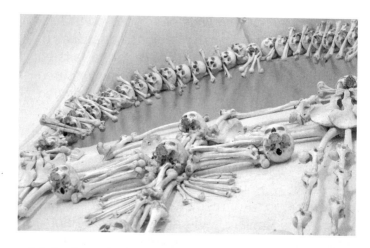

Interior views of a Catholic chapel (bone house) near Prague

removed from the catacombs and placed in a porphyry basin beneath the high altar."[67] The foundation of this church consists of hundreds upon hundreds of skeletons, and the high altar was built upon this.

It could be said that the beliefs and practices of the Catholic Church are really founded on bones, that it is a cult of the dead. This statement is justified by the fact that this veneration of relics is an intensification of a pagan cult. Generally we can conclude that much found in the Catholic Churches, almost all their customs, stems from paganism. We not only find its roots in paganism, but beyond this, the Catholic Church greatly increased the use of paganism. These relic customs were not known to such extent in paganism.

Perhaps we should question of whether any such customs and rites or cults come up in the teachings of Jesus of Nazareth at all. We would not find a single point in common! And a repeated comparison would be worthwhile: What did Jesus, the Christ, teach, and what does the Catholic Church teach?

Jesus said: "*Let the dead bury their dead. But you, follow Me*" (Mt.8:22).
And there is also a passage that reads:
And one of them, a lawyer, asked him a question to test him. Teacher, which is the great com-

mandment in the law? And he said to him, You shall love the Lord your God with all your heart and with all your soul and with all your mind. This is the great and first commandment. And a second is like it: You shall love your neighbor as yourself. On these two commandments depend all the law and the prophets. (Mt.22:35-40)

So, where did all the rest come from and what should it serve?

Some things are already known about this. Even the prophets of the Old Covenant, for instance, Jeremiah, knew that all this comes from paganism. For example, he said:

For the customs of the peoples are vanity. A tree from the forest is cut down and worked with an axe by the hands of a craftsman. They decorate it with silver and gold; they fasten it with hammer and nails so that it cannot move. Their idols are like scarecrows in a cucumber field, and they cannot speak; they have to be carried, for they cannot walk. Do not be afraid of them, for they cannot do evil, neither is it in them to do good. (Jer.10:3-5)

So, even the prophets said that such customs were all hullabaloo, and that the people of God should not surround themselves with such statues or put together such objects made of wood, silver and gold for their belief, because all that is done by the pagans. Clearly, the Catholic Church closed rank with pagan cults, and not with the true prophets of God.

Dark superstition – still today:
A relic in the pectoral cross of bishops,
a relic in every altar... Dogma: "Anyone who does not accept all the whole of church tradition..." – is for all practical purposes, in hell

Many a guileless person would like to say that these relics of dark superstition belong to a distant past. But it is particularly shocking to see that actually, it is all much closer to us than we would like to think. Recently a visit was made to the museum holding the cathedral treasures of Würzburg, Germany. There, the insignia of the current bishops, in use right up until today, was on display.

For example, the "pectoral cross." Since the 12th century, every bishop has to wear a certain pectoral cross. Already in the 4th century, it was an amulet, a vessel that held a relic. And to this day, it is stipulated that a relic must be contained in this pectoral cross. In this and similar ways, these rituals and insignia are carried into the present and passed on.

A relic is also worked into every altar. A Catholic altar is fully consecrated only when it contains a relic.

What would a Catholic believer say, who did not know that such bones or other sacrosanct corpse pieces continue to rot away in the altar of the church which he may be visiting Sunday after Sunday?

Here, a thoughtful contemporary would ask: Do the people really have to believe in this cult of relics? And if it is not accepted by the so-called faithful, that is, if the people do not believe in it, what then?

We have already referred to the fact that it was particularly the power of relics that had to be believed. There is a dogma that all-embracingly declares the following: *"Any one does not accept the whole of the Church's tradition, both written and unwritten – anathema sit."* (Neuner-Roos, No. 78) So this means that the person who doesn't even know about this tradition, or who doesn't accept even a single component of this tradition, not believing it to be true, is already damned, without even knowing it. According to the Catholic Church, he already has one foot in hell, even without being aware of it.

But doesn't this concern almost all Catholics? It is hard to believe that every Catholic even knows all the dogmas and traditions of their church. Consequently, they are supporting a church that has long since damned them.

Perhaps we should clarify what it actually means to be eternally damned. Mostly we simply repeat the words, and are rather scandalized. But we become aware of the extent of it only when we realize what it really means: To eternally, forever more, suffer in the fire of unspeakable torment, and never be released from it. The Church teaches that there is no end to this torment, simply because one doesn't believe the one or other dogma. Recently, by the way, this is also the consequence when a couple lives together without a marriage certificate. Just a while ago, Benedict XVI proclaimed that marriage without a certificate is not compatible with the teachings of this Church, that is, it is a grave sin. And according to the dogma of eternal damnation, the one who dies in this condition of sin falls victim to the eternal fires of hell.

However, let it also be said that the Church is not shy to industriously collect money from the many who don't believe in all their dogmas, even though it explains to them that they are damned forever, because they do not believe everything that it proclaims.

Who is sitting on the Chair of Peter?
Tolstoy knew very well
who had founded the Church...

This is what the Church proclaims. Who believes that God commanded them to do this? Who would believe such a thing? No normal person would believe that Jesus, the Christ, or God, our Father, would have conveyed such a thought, such a mandate, to the

Church. If God is the love, then He is love. Love forgives, love pardons, love carries, but the Church damns! Who is sitting on the Chair of Peter here?

Leo Tolstoy, a great Russian author, said it very clearly in his story: "The Resurrection of Hell." This story was first published by his son after his death. It tells that after the event on Calvary, when Jesus died on the cross, the devil was banned into the deepest depths of hell. Thus, he was fettered, because after this time people strove to put the teachings of Jesus of Nazareth into practice. There was less fighting; the people reconciled with each other, and the devil had nothing more to do. Hell was empty. And then, after a long time, there was suddenly a lot of noise in hell and several devils came in joyfully with torches and Beelzebub demanded, pointing upward: "*What's going on there?*"[68] And they replied: "*Just what was and now always will be.*" They had put hell back into business again. When the devil asked how they did this, the second highest devil said "*... I invented 'The Church.'*"

Leo Tolstoy then described how this happened, that by inventing the Church, fighting started again among the people, that an elite class had been formed again that exploited others, and that the state exploited others as well, and in this way, the beginnings of early Christianity were destroyed, resulting in even more crime than before.

When the devil heard: "*I invented 'The Church',*" he said: "*What is 'The Church'*"? He didn't know. And the second highest devil answered with the following:

One can imagine the church in this way: When these hypocrites utter untruths and suspect that they will not be believed, they always call upon God to be their witness. This, in essence, is "The Church" but I built in another wrinkle. Those who call themselves "The Church" convince themselves that they cannot go wrong, so they convince themselves that they cannot and must not repudiate their lies. This greatest of lies is what they call "infallibility." I taught these pathetic men that God, to ensure that he should not be misunderstood, gave power to certain men, and to those to whom they chose to transfer this power, that they alone could infallibly interpret his teachings. So these men, who collectively call themselves 'The Church' regard themselves as possessing the truth, not because what they have passed on is good or reasonable, but simply because they see themselves as the only true heirs of the disciples, their hated master, and finally of God himself.

So, Tolstoy's opinion was that the devil founded the Church. And that Tolstoy wasn't just shooting in the dark is shown in the following formulation of the Catholic Church in Neuner-Roos:

Hence also the meaning of the sacred dogmas is perpetually to be retained which our Holy Mother Church has once declared; nor is that meaning ever to be departed from under the pretence or pretext of a deeper comprehension of them. ... (No. 48)

And, as already quoted: "*Any one does not accept the whole of the Church's tradition, both written and unwritten – anathema sit*" (No. 78).

In No. 351, we also read: "*... It is to be held as a matter of faith that no one can be saved outside the Apostolic Roman Church. It is the only ark of salvation and anyone who does not enter it must sink in the flood.*"

Logically, this means that all other religions deserve eternal damnation. The great world religions are, for example, Hinduism, Buddhism, Islam, Jainism, Confucianism, Judaism, Taoism, or even all the Protestant and other denominations that are not Catholic. It has always been said that this statement was weakened at the Vatican Council, but this is not borne out. We can read what was decided at the Vatican Council, in Neuner-Roos: "*Hence they could not be saved who, knowing that the Catholic Church was founded as necessary by God through Christ, would refuse either to enter it or to remain in it*" (No. 417, German Edition).

But who of the Protestants all over the world does not know of the Catholic Church? Everyone knows the Catholic Church. This means that this sentence holds true for all people except at most, some isolated tribes in the rainforest of Papua New Guinea or the Amazon basin, who really don't know that a Catholic Church exists. But for all others it holds true: According to the Church, they are damned.

Getting back to the question: Who is sitting on the Chair of Peter? The founder of the Protestant Lutheran Church, Martin Luther, wrote an answer in the Smalcald Articles in 1537:

… all things which the Pope, from a power so false, mischievous, blasphemous, and arrogant, has done and undertaken, have been and still are purely diabolical affairs and transactions … the holy Christian Church can exist very well without such a head, and it would certainly have remained better if such a head had not been raised up by the devil … This teaching shows forcefully that the Pope is the very Antichrist, who has exalted himself above, and opposed himself against Christ because he will not permit Christians to be saved without his power … the Pope's teaching, where it is best … is nothing other than the devil himself, because above and against God he urges his falsehoods concerning masses, purgatory, the monastic life, one's own works and divine worship … and condemns, murders and tortures all Christians

who do not exalt and honor these abominations above all things. Therefore, just as little as we can worship the devil himself as Lord and God, we can endure his apostle, the Pope, or Antichrist, in his rule as head and lord. For in the Council we will stand ... before the Pope and devil himself, who intends to listen to nothing, but merely to condemn, to murder and to force us into idolatry...[69]

That is what the founder of the Lutheran Church has to say about the pope. And even though this was never retracted, the Protestant churches tend to curry favor with the Catholic Church. Why? Maybe because the Protestant Lutheran Church also still has a lot of paganism in it. The Protestants did not take over the cult of Mary and relics, but they did take over a lot of other things that are pagan. For example, the altars in the churches are a pagan concept, a pagan practice. The pulpit existed already in the Isis cult. And the early Christians did not have communion in such a ritualized form as has been developed in the Catholic and Lutheran churches. They celebrated a feast of love together, at which they ate with each other and at which the poor were also fed. It is only later that it became ritualized and was turned into something called the Sacrifice of the Mass, a meal of sacrifice, which also existed in pagan cults.

Luther took this over as well as many other aspects. But above all, the Protestant-Lutherans took over the main component, namely, that of the priests, where a human being presumes to stand between an individual and God. It is a central aspect of Catholic teaching, that you can get into heaven only when you believe what another person tells you. And the Protestant Church also took over this superstition: Only the priests can mediate salvation for you. Whereby they are also contradicting their own Bible again, because it says there: *"For there is one God, and there is one mediator between God and men"* and now it comes, not the priests, but it says in the Bible, *"the man Jesus Christ."* There's no talk at all about priests in 1 Tim. 2:5.

Although they adopted a lot of things from the Catholic Church which, in turn, took from paganism, none of this is going to do the Protestants any good, because according to Catholic teaching, if they do not adopt the central doctrines of Catholic faith in their entirety, then all Protestants are damned.

We have now heard a lot about eternal damnation, about hell, and such atrocities. On the one hand, the Catholic Church acknowledges that man bears within an immortal soul; on the other hand, it proclaims that the one who doesn't believe in its dogma will be destroyed. So the life created by God will be destroyed, if the person doesn't believe in the dogmas of this organization.

Of itself, hell is a thought, of which we must say that if just one person lands in eternal damnation and stays there, that would be a victory over God, because God created this life. God is a God of love and if only one person remains eternally damned, then God would be vanquished. So therefore, this teaching of hell and of eternal damnation is a blasphemy against God.

But when we question this more exactingly, it is often denied or played down by the Catholics. For example, a German Catholic newspaper (*Weltbild*, 20/96: "Ewig Einsam"), has a forum for the Catholics to ask questions and receive answers and there it says: *"How should one talk about hell these days?"* And the answer is: *"There is a thesis that hell means for a person that he simply ceases to exist. He is no more."*

Does this means that suddenly there is a brand new interpretation? What's behind this thought that the person shall no longer exist?

They're not saying it's a dissolution into Nirvana, where the energy still remains, but that the person dissolves into nothing. What is "nothing"? Is there such a thing as nothing if everything is energy? The law of God knows no such thing as decay, or dissolution or disappearing or ceasing to exist. Instead, it knows only transformation, evolution and growing into higher forms of being. So behind such a statement, that a being simply ceases to exist, there is either a profound lack of spiritual knowledge, or perhaps the desire to destroy the creation of God.

The Catholic Church also claims in its Catechism that the Church is "necessary for salvation." (No. 846) This means that for the salvation of a person it is necessary to be in this church. If he is not in this church, then he will not attain salvation; he is damned.

This is even written up in a dogma, also found in Neuner-Roos:

The Holy Roman Church, founded through the word of our Lord and Redeemer, firmly believes, confesses and proclaims that no one outside of the Catholic Church, neither pagan nor Jew, nor non-believer or one separated from the unity will take part in eternal life, but will rather fall victim to the eternal fire, which is prepared for the devil and his angels, if before his death he does not join it (the church). (No. 381, German edition)

Protestant-Lutheran doctrine:
God has pre-determined, that is,
has foreseen, who goes to heaven
and who goes to hell

It has become clear that according to Catholic doctrine, Protestants, for example, will fall victim to the eternal fires of eternal damnation. Now, as a Protestant, a person could deny this by saying that he doesn't believe in this dogma, and therefore has nothing to worry about, perhaps even quoting the Bible: "*Come out of her, my people, lest you take part in her sins, lest you share in her plagues.*" (Rev. 18:4) However, what a Protestant-Lutheran person doesn't know is that he might be jumping from the pot into the frying pan. For although it is not openly stated today, the Protestant-Lutheran Church teaches that a person is predestined. According to the arbitrary will of God, a part of mankind is promised salvation and the other part falls victim to eternal damnation, without being able to do anything about it. Such a doctrine is actually even more perverse than that of the Roman-Catholic Church. So, Protestant-Lutheran belief surely is not a way out of this dilemma.

To shed more light on this, we quote from an article published in "Quodlibet Online Journal of Christian Theology and Philosophy" written by Ken Ristau and titled: "Concerning the Will: An historical and analytical essay examining Martin Luther's treatise 'The Bondage of Will.'"[70]

God is all-powerful and therefore, God's will is alone immutable. Any person, therefore, that appeals to the freedom of human will attempts to usurp for themselves an attribute that belongs only to God ... God freely chooses to create our present reality and likewise, He freely sustains this reality. In fact, reality does not exist except by the will of God ... In this respect, one realizes why Luther cannot ascribe free will to any created being. For Luther, the concept of free will requires total autonomy that can only exist as an attribute of the Divine, whose will is not subject to any other will. God, in effect, creates the ability to will. God alone has free will. As Luther states, it follows, therefore, that 'free-will' is obviously a term applicable only to the Divine Majesty; for only He can do, and does (as the Psalmist sings) 'whatever he wills in heaven and earth' (Ps. 135:6).[71]

In Luther's theology, the will of God is not contingent and so likewise, the foreknowledge of God is also not contingent. For whatever God wills, he foreknows and so, whatever He foreknows must, by necessity, happen ... Luther ... asserts, though not at any length, that the grace of God is a gift given only to the elect, to those whom God by his foreknowledge has predes-

*tined to become his children … "So utterly does
grace refuse to allow any particle or power of
'free-will' to stand beside it"* [72] *and at the conclusion of his work where he declares: "So, if we
believe that Satan is the prince of this world,
ever ensnaring and opposing the kingdom of
Christ with all his strength, and that he does not
let his prisoners go unless driven out by the
power of the Divine Spirit, it is again apparent
that there can be no 'free-will.'"* [73]

So, clearly a person doesn't need a church. Because whether it is foreseen or predestined, if it happens anyway, then I must have really taken leave of
my senses, if I still pay into and support this institution.

*A church that denies the free will
of the people denies the foundation
of the legal order.
A paradox in effect*

The absurdity of this doctrine becomes particularly
clear when we apply these statements to specific inci-
dents. Imagine a court case, where someone has
committed a crime, and the perpetrator of the crime
says: "Well, even before I was born, God decided
that I would be a bad person or would commit a bad

crime. So you can't condemn me for this." What would the judge have to say about this?

Most likely, it would be for him as it is for most Protestants: He wouldn't know a thing about it. For the Protestants "believe," but for the most part, they do not really know <u>what</u> they believe in. So the judge would most likely simply ignore this objection

However, this remains an interesting paradox that is pre-programmed into the teachings of the Protestant-Lutheran Church and which undermines every legal system. A church that denies a person's freedom of will in ethical matters, and that says, as did Luther that: "*we are captives, bond slaves to Satan and by nature 'children of wrath.'*"[74] is basically denying the foundation of our legal system, including our constitution, which assumes that every person has the freedom to develop according to his personal decisions, to shape his life according to his ethical standards. All this is ruled out when we take Luther's teaching seriously.

Our whole legal system could not function. No one could be sentenced for a crime, since right from the beginning the perpetrator of the crime lacks any guilt in the matter.

Basically, we have a senseless condition of unfree "marionettes of God." Although God is freedom, a God of love, an image of man is being instilled that turns the creations of God into marionettes, something that God never created.

So do we need a legal system at all if we are all marionettes? The one is condemned to evil and the other to good, the one for heaven, the other for hell. According to Luther, we cannot do otherwise. So then, do we need a legal system?

The state couldn't even function according to the Lutheran principle, so it is simply ignored. And there is one thing we shouldn't forget: If the jury or judge were to deny the free will of the accused just as Luther did, they would have to deny their own and then declare themselves incapable of sound judgment, and with this, the whole system would fall apart.

From a logical point of view, the next question we could ask would be if we even need a legal system at all, since according to Protestant teaching, a person is pre-destined, and Catholic doctrine states: "If you don't believe, you are eternally damned." If I am eternally damned, why do I need a court decision?

Catholic theologians would counter by saying that the legal order in the world should see to it that a certain order is maintained. Order for whom? For those who have already been damned?

The caste of priests determines
what takes place in the state
– as long as the people allow this.
A dictatorship tries to rule over
a democracy

If we look very closely at the Catholic doctrine, above all, the statements in the books of Moses, which according to Catholic doctrine are the "true word of God" and which the New Testament is said to "shed light" on, then we actually don't need a legal system because in the end, the priests always have the last word. And so, we could say that this legal system is merely a cloak that is draped about oneself when necessary, while in actuality, the Catholic Church says what should be done, and the world order should do what the Church wants. This is how the national or state legitimized order of law appears in church doctrine. One could also say that democracy, where power starts with the people, should be maintained for the sake of appearances. In reality, it is the caste of priests of the prevailing religion that wants to determine what is done.

We are reminded of what was done with Jesus of Nazareth. Who was it that killed Him? It wasn't the Roman occupational authority, the world power at that time; instead, it was the caste of priests. The question may have sounded rather strange: Do we need worldly judges? The answer could be: According to the Bible and church doctrines, we need them so that the caste of priests have a cover for their operations of violence.

Whether we call it the Lutheran Church or the Catholic Church, the government, in any case, should be their long arm, the one that carries out their policies as long as the people allow this.

This is also rather ingeniously stated in the book by Neuner-Roos (No. 349): *"We decree that the Holy Apostolic See and the Roman Pontiff have primacy in the whole world."*

Wouldn't one have to say: The people are led to believe in democracy, but in reality, isn't it a dictatorship of the Church behind democracy? Consider the fact that the Church demands of its faithful in every situation – be it private or professional – that Christian doctrine prevail as determined by church doctrine. With this, the ideology of an organization is being placed above the state legal system. Since it is a totalitarian ideology, which has nothing in common with democracy, one could justifiably say that here a dictatorship is attempting to rule over a democracy.

The imperative sentence of the
Catholic Church is applied in public life:
"We determine what is Christian!"

Of course, one must always differentiate between imperative sentences and the question whether these imperative sentences can realistically be exercised. Totalitarian imperative sentences from the Catholic pagan church are rather dangerous simply as imperative sentences.

Of course, many may say, "But in reality, they aren't put into practice!" It is interesting to note that Cardinal Meissner of Cologne recently demanded that the German political party, the Christian Democratic Union cross the C out of its name. Not because the CDU, as well as the Catholic Church, have nothing to do with Christ, but because, as he said: "We determine what is Christian!" Meissner let it be known that the party does not conform to his strict reactionary concepts. (Protestant Press Service: June 5, 2005) So apparently, this imperative sentence of the Church is not only on paper, but is also put into practice.

If anyone has any doubt about this, we recommend the book by Gabriele titled, "For Experienced Analysts: Discover the Truth. The Church and State Authority and the Justice of God."[75] With impressive conciseness and clarity, this book explains how these mechanisms function. According to it, the strings of a democratic state are being pulled by the caste of priests.

After all the absurdities that have been discussed here on pagan faith in the churches, we would like to quote a brief excerpt from this book. On page 75 it says:

> More and more people are critical toward church belief. Originally they equated God with the Church. But because they are no longer in agreement with the Church, they are now also doubting the existence of God. But which God? The God whom the churches taught about and still do? God is not the "God" of the churches! Christ is not the "Christ" of church doctrine! If the Spirit of eternal truth had not come at this time in His word, many would actually not know who God or who Christ is and what we should think of Him. They would not know that they can grow closer to Him and understand Him by turning to Him, who dwells in their inner being. Jesus taught that the Kingdom of God is in us. He taught us to go to a quiet chamber: "But when you pray, go into your room and shut the door and pray to your Father who is in secret; and your Father who sees in secret will reward you." (Mt.6:6)

*

Dear readers, if you are among those people who can no longer believe in the God of the churches and the Christ of the churches, then try out what Jesus taught us. Original Christians create a quiet room where they can withdraw to pray – it can simply be a small, nicely arranged corner in a room. But this can also be done by going into nature, by listening to the sounds of nature, by becoming quiet in the process, and praying to God, our Father, in this way. Soon, you can experience that this is the quickest way to draw closer to God in you.

*Did you find this picture to be a particularly perverse
form of the derision of Jesus, the Christ? Well, it is an antenna
near the Vatican in Rome.*

One last word ...

For anyone who doesn't yet know who is concealed behind the Chair of Peter, may he let this picture move him.

The demonic can be recognized not only in doctrines and dogmas, in the cult of idolatry and the rites of the Catholic Church – which, as a whole, totally opposes the teachings of Jesus, the Christ – but also in countless external symbols. Most people often misjudge the blasphemous message contained in such symbols, because these unsuspecting contemporaries don't know anything about their true significance and their pagan character – and don't think about them. Aside from that, most people wouldn't dare to think that the so-called "representative of God," who presents himself as "holy" and "Christian," and his entourage are capable of anything really bad, even though the facts from the cruel history of the Church speak a clear language.

The true mindset of the occupant of the Chair of Peter and those who serve him is shown in fully undisguised form in the misshapen figure with which someone "decorated" an antenna in Rome. It is the most horrible depiction of Jesus, the Christ, that anyone can imagine. Isn't contempt expressed in this horrid caricature, not totally unconcealed, as well as hatred, scorn, mockery, blasphemy and the like?

An Original Christian formulated his feelings as follows:

In my eyes the Vatican, the Holy See, and those who inspire it, are, with such a cross, symbolizing the anticipated defeat of the divine and the victory of the anti-Christ – as if they would say: Now we are trumpeting out into the world what WE want! But you have to be silent; you are dead and should stay dead and not get in our way, because we use your name to deceive the people and lead them astray. And so, we are making you into our servant. We are the masters of this world! Our voice is the cross upon which we have hung you again. And the many who follow us, subjugating themselves to us, will help us to the final victory.

But no matter how hard the ecclesiastical servants of idolatry try to withhold the living, speaking and near God from mankind – they will not succeed. For Christ lives! And He does not remain silent.

He, the great eternal Spirit of love and peace, is very close to each and every one. Since His words "It Is Finished" on the cross of Golgotha, He is present in the innermost part of every person's soul as light and power – and everyone can turn to Him at any time, without priests, dogmas, rites, ceremonies and the like. Christ helps; He heals, and He leads people into a life in the Spirit of God, which fulfills and makes us happy from within.

At all times the Spirit of the Christ of God has given revelations according to His promise: *"I have yet many things to say to you, but you cannot bear them now. When the Spirit of truth comes, he will guide you into all the truth ..."* (Jn.16:12). During this time, Christ has spoken and speaks through His prophetess, Gabriele. He gives instructions and detailed teachings for all aspects of human life and beyond that, explanations about the great interrelationships of the material and fine-material cosmos. Since God is absolute love, freedom and unity and thus, neither punishes His children nor forces them into anything, each one is also free to accept His divine word for the present time, or not. Whoever wants to can inform himself about this.

Letters to the Pope

After the election of Cardinal Ratzinger to the papacy, an Original Christian wrote him an extensive letter. Several weeks later, this letter had still received no answer, so a second letter was written, which till now has also remained unanswered.

Both texts are printed in their entirety on the following pages.

May 2, 2005

Honorable Pope Benedict,

Please do not hold the salutation I have used against me! I find it very difficult to address a human being as "Holy Father" or "Your Holiness." I am not turning to you as a member of your church, but simply as a brother in Christ.

Perhaps I may start by mentioning that we have already met one another, under quite critical circumstances. As Archbishop of Munich and Freising, you had introduced disciplinary measures against a rebellious local priest who refused to deliver his Peter's Pence. And this man turned to me of all people, as a lawyer, to help prevent his dismissal via the use of

189

legal channels. The dispute over church law turned into a personal meeting, during which you showed understanding, and which ultimately led to an amicable agreement. The priest was thankful to his cardinal and the lawyer was impressed by the cardinal's readiness to reconcile. Considering your eventful life, of course, I find it very improbable that you still remember this encounter. Presumably just as little, that you may have heard that on the television program "Dieci minuti" on RAI UNO, a German jurist appeared who presented a religious movement that refers itself back to early Christianity. The Munich lawyer of that time has meanwhile become a (hopefully) modest God-seeker within the circle of an Original Christian community, which tries to understand the teachings of Jesus of Nazareth and to put them into practice in daily life without church dogmas and rites.

By referring to this effort, I will allow myself to pose several questions to the newly elected pope of the Roman-Catholic Church. This may seem presumptuous, but Christ does not differentiate between high-ranking and low-ranking persons. And since it concerns fundamental questions about being Christian, these should not be discussed in a closed circle – which is why I also allow myself to write this as an open letter.

The first question was once posed by yourself: As Bishop of Limburg, Franz Kamphaus recently reported in the "Frankfurt Allgemein Newspaper" that during the mid 1960s, you, already a conciliar theologian, pointed out that as pope it is dangerous to let oneself be called "Holy Father." You stated that the words of Jesus are against this: "*... you have one Father, who is in heaven. Neither be called masters, for you have one master, the Christ*" (Mt.23:9-10). For many this may seem merely a formality. But as you said yourself, "*The words of Jesus are against this.*" This is why the question arises in terms of how seriously does the new pope take the words of Jesus, the Christ, when he, too, lets himself be called "Holy Father" and lets the people kneel before him?

The same question also applies to the Church as an institution, when, despite its bloody past, it continues to view itself as the one and only true institution of salvation in Christendom, and which, under threat of spiritual punishment, requisitions its members already as babies and holds on to them as adults. In your much-read "Introduction to Christendom,"[76] you wrote already in 1968 that in view of the history of the Church, you could understand: "*Dante's terrible vision of the Babylonian whore sitting in the Church's chariot*" (p. 339).

The consequences to be drawn from this can be found in the Revelation of John, who, referring to the whore of Babylon, advised: "*Come out of her my people, lest you share in her sins!*" (Rev.18:4).

But anyone who wants to follow this advice is threatened by the Church with the horrible punishment of eternal damnation.

Whoever seeks advice in your theology for the solution to this conflict between salvation in Christ and calamity in the Church receives paradoxical information:

> Because of the Lord's devotion, never more to be revoked, the Church is the institution sanctified by him forever, an institution in which the holiness of the Lord becomes present among men. But it is really and truly the holiness of the Lord that becomes present in her and that chooses again and again as the vessel of its presence – with a paradoxical love – the dirty hands of men. It is holiness that radiates as the holiness of Christ from the midst of the Church's sin … One could actually say that precisely in her paradoxical combination of holiness and unholiness the Church is in fact the shape taken by grace in this world. (pp. 341-42)

I am not a learned theologian. Perhaps that is why I cannot avoid the impression that this is an intellectual game, in which things are turned upside down: The Apriori is no longer *the Lord,* but the Church; He becomes the vehicle of an organization, which because of His *"devotion, never more to be revoked"* also remains holy when it turns away from Him. At the end of your deduction, you write that "*this unholy holiness of the Church has in itself something infinitely comforting about it*" (p. 343).

Honorable Pope Benedict, what would Jesus of Nazareth have to say about so much paradox? Would He not refuse to have your church call itself the "mystical body of Christ"? And particularly since, according to your paradox of the "unholy holiness," it was and is allowed to do as it pleases – also during the centuries of the Crusades and Inquisition, during which it drew its trail of blood throughout the history of the world? Does not this motto "once holy, always holy" make the Church unpredictable for the future, not to say dangerous?

In your book, you protest that:
> the criticism of the Church adopts that tone of rancorous bitterness ... accompanied only too often by a spiritual hollowness ... in which she is regarded only as a political instrument whose organization is felt to be pitiable or brutal, as if the real function of the Church did not lie beyond the organization, in the comfort of the Word and of the sacraments ... (p. 343)

This may very well be, but was not the "real function" buried by the "non-function" long ago? Considering the imperial cut and power structure of your church in history and at present, how do you justify to the people its spiritual claim before God and in the name of Jesus Christ?

Allow me to presume for a moment myself as the Nazarene's lawyer, in order to pose a few more awkward questions regarding this: Do you find it compatible with the teachings of Jesus that the Church continues to keep the enormous wealth, which it acquired over the course of centuries and partly through deception and violence? Or would it not be time to act to relieve the hunger and misery in the Third World with it? What would Jesus of Nazareth advise?

What would Jesus of Nazareth think of the unfoldment of pomp and splendor that the world experienced with the death of your predecessor and your own enthronement? Admittedly Jesus knew how to celebrate at the proper time – just think of the wedding at Canaan. But in a world in which 40,000 children starve to death day after day, the glistening pomp of gold and crimson in the name of Jesus takes on questionable proportions. The Church used its festivities as acts of state of the Catholic world mission. But in the loud media spectacle the chance for spirituality turned rather into a mass psychosis, in which the "representatives of God" were paid homage as idols, while Christ became a mere decoration as the crucified one. Just as an aside: Why is He still hanging on the cross, even though He resurrected long ago?!

Perhaps with a more broadminded way of looking at things, one could overlook much that is irritating in the way of the external discrepancies between the carpenter and the rich Church. More painful is the denial of Jesus by the central dogma of the Church. Is it not dreadful that many church Christians become uncertain when asked why Christ became a human being and why He had to die such a terrible death? Someone who rummages about in his memories of Catholic religion class will falteringly answer that this sacrifice was necessary in order to reconcile God with mankind. But anyone who seriously reflects upon this answer, his heart must skip a beat: This must be a dreadful God who is so offended that He demands human sacrifice as compensation, and, at that, His own Son.

Such an image of God frightens many people and also makes Jesus of Nazareth suspect.

But whoever opens the catechism of his church (perhaps in the hope that he was mistaken) will be confirmed in this nightmare: He reads that *"the Father handed his Son over to sinners in order to reconcile us with himself,"* that Jesus *"makes himself an offering for sin,"* that his *"blood ... was poured out for many for the forgiveness of sins,"* and that he *"made satis-faction for our sins to the Father."* For about a thousand years, this doctrine has gnawed on the roots of human trust in God and a plausible belief in the meaning of the life of Jesus. You also saw this dilemma as a theologian, when you write of the *"sinister light,"* into which this doctrine of the image of God immerses. (p. 233) Therefore, you attempt with much theological eloquence to qualify the downright satanic components of this to Anselm of Canterbury, basically going back to Paul's "theory of satisfaction." You emphasize that it was not confirmed by the gospel. When in the letter to the Hebrews it says that Jesus accomplished expiation through his blood, this is not *"to be understood as a material gift, a quantitatively measurable means of expiation,"* but simply as *"the concrete expression of a love of which it is said that it extends to the end."* (p. 287)

A person who believes in a loving God and takes Jesus' message seriously can only assume that His death is not a new pagan sacrifice, but the expression of His unconditional loyalty to His mission: to proclaim the Kingdom of God to mankind and to bring His Kingdom of Peace to the earth. But when one is in agreement about the true mission of Jesus, why has your church not dissociated itself in its doctrine long ago from the pagan, completely falsified myth of sacrifice? The presently valid version of the Catechism of the Catholic Church was published in the year 1992. Can a church, which in its Catechism, in thousands of devotions and prayers, lets the Son of God be revered as a necessary human sacrifice, still seriously base itself on Him?

In addition, how can a church make the formulation of "Lamb of God, who takes away the sins of the world," into a religious mantra, and simultaneously threaten with eternal damnation all those who stumble over the casuistry of its doctrine of mortal sin? During my youth, this could still happen, when someone read a book on the index, or kissed a girl too passionately or did not appear at mass on Sunday two or three times. Things may not be so bad today, but according to Church doctrine, the majority of church Christians are still moving quite close to the abyss of eternal hell.

With this, I am not supporting a "Dictatorship of Relativism," but am raising an objection in the name of Jesus and of His Father who infinitely loves us all, whose almighty kindness is insulted when one implies that He eternally damns the majority of mankind. The early Christian theologian Origen still knew that at the end of time everything would be good and all people would return to God ("Apokatastasis"); but the Council of Constantinople put an end to this in 553 – not because there were serious spiritual or theological grounds against his teachings; instead, it was mainly because the East-Roman Emperor Justinian wanted to nip a religious quarrel in the bud about the pre-existence of the human soul and the redemption of all souls and people by Christ. This is why he did not shilly-shally long and presented the assembly with anathemas against Origen and thus against an essential part of the Good News of Christ. The Roman state Church took leave of His message about a loving Father-God who damns no one, but who will bring back all souls and people, all of fallen creation, into the eternal homeland – with the help of the Redeemer-deed of Jesus, which enables all human beings to turn back and change their ways. Since then, the Church has had their sharpest weapon in hand: the threat of eternal damnation, which it used very effectively over the next 1500 years. It also became the basis of the Inquisition and of the Crusades, costing the lives of millions of people.

How can a church still base itself on Jesus of Nazareth, when in the most important questions, it does not orient itself to Him, but to other teachers? And men such as Paul, Canterbury and Justinian were by no means the only ones. Only the fewest of Catholics know that the Apostles' Creed was not formulated by early Christian followers of Jesus, not even by theologians, but by other Roman emperors aside from Justinian. This started already at the Council of Nicaea in the year 325, which Emperor Constantine had called to smooth out the first big theological debate, the quarrel between Arius and Athanasius: about whether Jesus, the Christ, was God Himself ("of the same substance as God") or the Son of God ("of a similar substance as the Father"). It was not a pious follower of Christ, but a (non-baptized) Roman Emperor, who decreed that Christ is "of the same substance as God," and who thus helped determine an essential aspect of the Catholic Creed, which is valid until today. Jesus may have said: *"The Father and I are one,"* but He did not say, I am "the true God of the true God," as the Church has prayed Sunday after Sunday, thanks to Constantine.

You know better than I that other articles of faith came into being in similar ways: for example, the dogma of the trinity and the dogma of the only true Church. Here, too, a Roman emperor, Theodosius I, in 381 at the Council of Constantinople, presumed to determine the doctrine by dictum. He convened the council, and one of his jurists, who was quickly baptized, consecrated as a priest and promoted to metropolitan, took over the leadership of the assembly, in order to juristically bring the dogma of trinity to paper without objections. At the same time, the Church was declared "holy" and "apostolic" and its means of grace were declared the instruments of salvation for the new state religion. What Theodosius and his jurist made final is until today a component of the creeds of all Christian denominations. However, it is not "Christian," because it did not come from Christ, but from the Roman-Catholic state Church.

Perhaps you would like to counter by wondering: Why a non-Catholic cares about this? After all he does not have to accept this creed. However, this objection is not valid as long as the Catholic Church does not renounce its claim to being the sole representation in matters pertaining to Christianity and does not acknowledge that church and Christianity are not identical. With this, I come to the troublesome question of the relationship of your church to Christians who are not counted among your members and who want to follow the Christ of God without church doctrine. To a certain extent, this pertains to your own field as the former Prefect of the Congregation for the Doctrine of the Faith in the succession of church officials of the Inquisition.

Recently, you did not deny this continuity; instead, you underlined it when in March of this year, you explained on Radio Berlin-Brandenburg: "Great Inquisitor is a historic decision, and somewhere, we stand in its continuity." This made us take notice, even more so the next sentence in which you remarked that one "must say" that the Inquisition was a progressive step, because nothing more could be condemned without inquisitio, which means, that investigations took place. I assume that you had in mind the nature of these "investigations," by which people were often cruelly tortured, when you said in the same interview that "the methods of that time could in part be criticized." Perhaps your statements in the interview were passed on in shortened form, since to me, they seem to make light of the whole thing.

At any rate permit me to question whether, and to what extent, the declaration of the Second Vatican Council on freedom of religion can be relied upon. This question arises not only because the Church allowed itself time until 1965 to separate itself from the right and the "duty to suppress moral and religious fallacies" (Pius XII). The council's explanation, in connection with other church documents, also gives reason for considerable doubt, when it insists that freedom of religion *"leaves untouched traditional Catholic doctrine on the moral duty of men and society (!?) toward the true religion and toward the one Church of Christ."* [77]

This always concerns not only a "moral," but also a legal duty, which the Church assumed in this connection. This is why it is frightening that until today the letter of Pius IX to the Munich-Freising Archbishop can still be found in the collection of the official doctrines. In this letter, the pope said about his Church:

"She must therefore with painstaking care remove and eradicate (?!) anything that is contrary to faith or in any way harmful to the salvation of souls." (Neuner-Roos, No. 352) As long as this text is not annulled, the Church's claim to having sole right of salvation remains a threat, which prompted Karl Jaspers to say that this ecclesiastical claim is *"constantly ready to ignite the pyres for heretics."* [78]

At this point, someone who lives as a Christian outside the Church can no longer limit himself to mere questions or requests. Here one must, in the name of Jesus and of human rights, demand that the Church get rid of the aggressive tinder of such doctrines once and for all. Since by definition reconciliation among Christians is a deep concern of yours, a papal stroke of the pen in "Neuner-Roos" should not be too difficult for you.

An honest "decree of tolerance" from the pope would have beneficial results in many ways: It would not only be an important contribution toward peace between different directions of faith. It is possible that it would also open doors within the Church for a gust of wind from the Holy Spirit, which, as we know, blows where it wills, and does not tolerate, in the long run, an approach that leads to narrow, theological-dogmatic concepts. Does it really occur to no one in Church circles that the early Christians not only had the gift of healing, but also the gift of prophecy, which is reported about several times in the Gospels? And that, with very few exceptions, the prophetic stream never appeared within the Church, but only outside its walls – and was instead persecuted with fire and sword there?

In any case, no one less than Karl Rahner wrote a complete treatise concerning the possibility of "private revelations." "Private" because they do not come from the mainstream churches, which do not believe anymore in revelations from the divine world, perhaps because here, too, it claims sole rights, in this case not only toward the people, but perhaps even toward the Spirit of God? Can one seriously imagine that God has remained silent for 2000 years, even though, at all times, He revealed Himself through the mouth of prophets?

There are many people who are convinced that today, too, a prophet lives among us, this time in the form of a woman, through whom a divine work of revelation and a worldwide Original Christian community has emerged. The one who unbelievingly waves this aside should not do this without a new look into your book that I have already quoted several times. Under the chapter heading "Doubt and Belief," you describe, based on Kierkegaard's parable of the clown and the burning circus, the situation of the believing one who alarms the fire department and is laughed at, because no one takes him seriously in his clown suit. In your text, the clown symbolizes the theologians. Perhaps one should at least for a moment, exchange him with the figure of a prophet. Then your words of the *"frustrating inability to break through accepted patterns of thought and speech…"* (p. 40) would be relevant in a new dimension. The "ignorant villagers," whom the clown encounters in Kierkegaard's parable, would then be the ignorant church folk, whom the prophet faces. In the "Dilemma of Faith," His revelation would be no weaker than the dogma of theologians, for as you so aptly write:

> *But however strongly unbelief may feel justified thereby, it cannot forget the eerie feeling induced by the words "Yet perhaps it is true." That "perhaps" is the unavoidable temptation it cannot elude … both the believer and the unbeliever share, each in his own way, doubt and belief, if they do not hide from themselves and from the truth of their being. Neither can quite escape either doubt or belief …* (pp. 46-47)

People have faced this dilemma of faith over and over again, every time they encountered a prophet. Most of them rejected the prophet, above all, the priests of the respective time. They have tradition in mind, and the prophets, on the other hand, have revolution in mind, which is why they are, by their very nature, suspect to the priests. Even when the Son of God appeared on earth, nothing changed – and just as little changed when later enlightened men and women, mystics and visionaries threatened to shake the Church's dogmatically entrenched structure of faith. Often their experience is reflected in Dostoyevsky's story "The Grand Inquisitor," with the reappeared Christ. There, the medieval prince of the Church said to him:

> *We have corrected Thy work and have founded it upon miracle, mystery and authority. And men rejoiced that they were again led like sheep … Why hast Thou come now to hinder us? … We are not working with Thee, but with him – that is our mystery. It's long – eight centuries – since we have been on his side and not on Thine. Just eight centuries ago, we took from him, the wise and mighty spirit in the wilderness, what Thou didst reject with scorn, that last gift he offered Thee, showing Thee all the kingdoms of the earth. We took from him Rome and the sword of Caesar, and proclaimed ourselves sole rulers of the earth …* [79]

It could be similar when a new prophet walks the earth, referring back to the buried teachings of Jesus and disregarding all the dogmas and rites, but who is ignored by the pope. Perhaps he is sent off with threats like the reappeared Christ in Dostoyevsky's story; perhaps he is ridiculed like the clown in Kierkegaard's parable, who calls for the fire department. The circus burns and rescue would be possible, if one would believe the call of alarm. If today, one were to not regard such calls to rescue from the divine-spiritual world as simply impossible, then even a skeptic would check it out, when he weighs the risks of doing this or not. If he checks it out and finds nothing prophetic in it, he can withdraw again and will have lost nothing – outside of a bit of time and energy. However, if he does not check it out and the prophetic is actually there, present, he would have lost everything by refusing to check it out.

As an example of the prophetic call of alarm for our time, I allow myself to include for you the book "The Great Cosmic Teachings of Jesus of Nazareth for His Apostles and Disciples Who Could Understand Them."[80] It is just a small part of a great work of revelation, in which mankind learns a great many things about the development of the earth and the life on our planet, about the interconnections of spirit and matter, of body and soul, of health and illness.

And not lastly, much is revealed about the life and teachings of the Nazarene, which had disappeared over the course of centuries. The Spirit of God sets straight what has been falsely taught, and in part kept silent, about Jesus of Nazareth. It also describes how Jesus loved the animals. The revelations provide answers about the meaning and purpose of our life on earth, about the true significance of Jesus' deed of redemption, about the validity of the law of cause and effect, about the nature of the continuing life of the soul after the body passes away, about the coming time of mankind, the emerging Kingdom of Peace and much more.

I do not know whether this letter will "get through" to you. If it is God's will, it will happen and you can then decide for yourself what you think of my questions and above all: whether you want to seriously examine the possibility of a new divine prophecy.

With this and all future important decisions of your life, I wish you God's blessing and the guidance of Christ.

In this spirit, I greet you as your brother in Christ,

July 19, 2005

Honorable Pope Benedict,

Allow me to refer to my extensive letter of May 2, 2005.

I do not know why I have received no answer of any kind until now. I cannot imagine that your state secretariat is so poorly organized. After all, time was found to give thanks for the teddy bear "Pope Benedict XVI" – in a "smiling" and "cordial" way, as it was emphasized. The pope as a teddy bear of "quality white curly mohair plush with a classic excelsior stuffing and elegant clothing" – is better received than the critical inquiry of a Christian, who bases himself on early Christianity and asks for an explanation on the ecclesiastical contradictions to the teachings of Jesus.

Now I have to guess whether my letter was tossed in the wastebasket by an over-eager prelate or whether it was considered on higher levels as an insult to his majesty. Just to make sure I am including the letter again. At the same time, I will send it to several cardinals in Germany and Italy, who perhaps may give my questions more attention. In any case, I will continue the correspondence indefinitely, by way of Internet, since questions of public interest are concerned here, given that your Church bases itself on Christ and many people are of the opinion that this is wrongly done. During the first 100 days of your time in office, you have made it clear that you apparently do not intend to lessen the distance between your Church and Jesus of Nazareth, not even little by little.

The hectic pace with which you want to canonize your predecessor proves just the opposite. As a theologian trained in history, you know better than I that the cult of saints and relics has not the least thing in common with Jesus. It sprang from ancient mystery cults, a primitive, physically oriented belief in spirits, which was later adopted by the Church. The Catholic cult of relics, in which bones of the deceased are revered, even being used for "miracle healings," proves itself as a perpetuation of pagan sorcery. Biblical findings conclude that holiness is due to One only, namely the "Lord of the Hosts." (Isaiah) The cult of a person practiced by the Roman-Catholic Church with their saints is a sacrilege, above all when you consider all those who have already been canonized or at least revered as saints – for example, Emperor Constantine, who exterminated his family, or Bernhard of Clairvaux, who called for murder and manslaughter, and many others, who have been canonized through the cruelty practiced in service of their Church.
While you speed up the canonization process, you are simultaneously allowing the intensification of so-

called exorcism. According to a report by the Catholic Press Agency, the ecclesiastical Regina Apostolorum University in Rome gives training courses in exorcism. The reason given by the university for its unusual class offering was the fact that "fascination with the devil" is growing. While one can still smile at many an aberration of the cult of saints, it gets bloody serious in the case of exorcism: Surely you are aware that people died recently or at least bore severe physical and mental damages from it. Many an aspect reminds one of African voodooism, in which they work with astral forces as do the Roman-Catholic exorcists. I would be so bold as to ask: In what world does the Vatican actually live? That no public outcry is raised when a pope of the 21st century lets such life-endangering magical rituals be practiced can only be explained by the simple fact that people have become accustomed to the medieval carryings-on of the Church or are simply indifferent to it. Could it be that magic is increasing in the same proportion that spirituality is declining? Someone practicing deep psychology would presumably verify that the more one represses one's own shadows, the more one encounters the devil.

Of the many positions stated by you during your first 100 days in office, one in particular begs for notice: Along with "pseudo marriages of persons of the same sex," "free unions" and "trial marriages" would also lead to a "trivialization of the body." At about the same time, Cardinal Lehmann of Germany made an appeal on television for organ donations – in full agreement with the prevailing church position. Where is there actually a greater banalization of the human body? When dying people are used as a warehouse for human spare parts and robbed of their still beating hearts and still functioning kidneys, in order to thus prolong for a few years the life of a person who is likewise deathly ill, thus mixing his body with that of another person? Or when two people live together without the blessing of the Church?

I do not want to seem impolite, but I really cannot spare you the question of whether you should not proceed more cautiously with verdicts about the trivialization of the human body, as long as the number of homosexual child-abusers in your Church still continues to rise and the banalization of sexuality in priest seminaries leads to orgies like those in St. Pölten exposed in 2004.

If you were to answer me, you would probably counter with the statement that of course, the Church frowns on this. Certainly you do this with words. Nevertheless, honorable Pope Benedict, you are under terrible suspicion of systematically protecting the culprits from criminal prosecution. In April of this year, a report went through the English press entitled "Pope

'Obstructed' Sex Abuse Inquiry,"[81] whereby you, as Prelate of the Congregation for the Doctrine of the Faith, are said to have sent a confidential letter to all Catholic bishops in which you requested them to keep investigations against child-abusers quiet, and at that, for ten years after the victim of abuse has attained legal age. According to German criminal law, this is clearly an act of abetting the prevention of prosecution according to § 258 of the German Penal Code. If you were not pope and thus a head of state, you would have to expect preliminary proceedings initiated by the public prosecutor's office when you visit Germany in the future. Presumably the prelates of your state secretariat will consider this statement improper and again look for the nearest wastepaper basket. But this simply is the legal situation. Or are the reports in the "Observer" and "Guardian" false reports? Why then, did the Vatican not disclaim them?

Apropos head of state: What do you have to say about the demand of 80 Catalonian priests that you should resign as "head of state"? The letter was published in the newspaper "La Vanguardia de Barcelona" on June 29, 2005. The authors, who were supported by several priest forums from southern and northern Catalonia, at the same time asked you to rehabilitate all theologians whom you silenced as Prelate of the Congregation for the Doctrine of the Faith. Those who wrote the letter based their demands on the desire that the Church again draw closer to the Gospel of Jesus. This is why they also condemn *"the spectacle surrounding the death of John Paul II and your election as pope,"* as being *"neither Christian nor constructive." "Even the presence of heads of states and governments – some of them promoters of wars, dictatorships and hunger – has nothing to do with Jesus of Nazareth, just as the hullabaloo of church authorities with their luxury and splendor."* Finally, the authors of the letter request that you no longer let yourself be called *"Holy Father, Pontifex Maximus and Your Holiness."*

The priests who expressed this are not opponents of the Church; instead, they feel a duty to the Nazarene. What would Jesus have had to say about this letter? And how does the resurrected Christ view this matter? Therefore, what you, who see yourself as the representative of Christ, will answer to this is of particular interest. Basically, you should agree with these Christ-friends. If you do not or if you consider the requests of your fellow brothers to be insubordination, you are acting as the opponent of God, even though directly after your election, you proclaimed that you wanted to work as "a modest servant in the vineyard of the Lord." When a person in one breath allows himself to be called Pontifex Maximus and Holy Father, it is probably difficult for him to not lose sight of reality. And when in addition, he still wants to speak in the name of Christ, then he is surely exposing his soul to quite a schizophrenic test of tensility.

Symptoms of such a split consciousness were recognized many times during the first 100 days of your pontificate.

Particularly with regard to your appeal after the terrorist acts in London. You called on the Moslems to *"stop in the name of God."* (CNN online July 11, 2005) A person has to have more than his fair share of ignorance to not be overcome with speechlessness here. Are you really not aware that one of your predecessors, Pope Urban II, called for the first Crusade against the Islamic world with the same words, "in the name of God," and promised every Crusader who sacrificed his life "in the battle against the pagans" that all his sins would be immediately forgiven?

The appeals of the pope 900 years ago are almost literally the same as the calls for jihad by the Islamic fundamentalists of today. What the Christians did then and during the following centuries to the Islamic world has not been forgotten until today. The leaders of Al-Quaida have expressly referred to the cruelty of the Christians who murdered and plundered in Jerusalem, to then conclude by "honoring the grave of the Redeemer." The terrible crimes of your Church poisoned world history already at that time. Your predecessor, John Paul II, did not seriously apologize for this; instead, he placed the blame on some Christians who had gone astray. The satanic energy that was released on the side of the Church against the Moslem world is hitting back today, at the entire western world. This does not in any way justify the cruel deeds in New York, Madrid or London. But when, of all people, the representative of that organization that bears the greatest guilt for the bloody embroilments over centuries of world history authoritatively calls toward the East for peace, then, for that part of Islam that reacts with suicide assassinations to the abasement by the West, this is like pouring oil onto the fire.

Would it not have been politically smarter and ethically long since called for, that the new pope take the opportunity to apologize for the many wounds that the so-called Christian western world has inflicted on the Islamic world? And that he then call for relieving their material need through energetic help, making available for this a part of the wealth of his Church (since much of it was acquired through a series of raids throughout the whole world); that he then strongly call on the American president and the British prime minister to seriously investigate the torture of and religious discrimination against Moslem prisoners, to punish those responsible and to stop it ...? Only then would a papal appeal for peace in the Middle and Far East no longer be seen as a provocation by inveterate crusaders. When the pope puts himself in the limelight as you did – and perhaps secretly harbors the illusion that he is still at the "helm of the globe" – then this concerns every contemporary, because we are all threatened by the anger and hatred of the terrorists, who may feel even more provoked by unfeeling appeals from Rome, even though old crimes and abasements hardly justify new acts of cruelty.

It can be that what is heard from you and seen of you may concern only the Catholics and members of the Church. But as long as the pope of this Church speaks over and over again in the name of "Christendom," everyone who is close to Jesus, the Christ, is concerned, and experiences how little ecclesiastical statements and behavior patterns have to do with Him. This is why I turn to you publicly. I will also do so in the future – even if my letters do not reach you or are ignored with your knowledge.

You must decide yourself whether in your world of papal holiness and infallibility you avoid critical questions and want to limit communication with the external world to safe dialogues of a diplomatic kind. When the German treasury secretary gets your blessing for a postage stamp, then he certainly does not tell you that he will gradually be unable to pay the billions in subsidies to your Church from state coffers. But a normal taxpayer like myself would point out to you that although the German taxpayers still annually subsidize with 14 billion Euro the church bureaucrats, from whom the faithful are leaving in droves, this cannot last much longer. And when in August the youth acclaim you in Cologne, then do not risk having a Catholic boy scout ask you why the Church so unconditionally protects life in an unborn state and then lets it be so freely destroyed after birth – for instance, in "just wars" or even by forbidding birth control, which brings hunger and misery, Aids and death, with it.

This is why you have to be confronted with such questions by normal contemporaries as myself, who feels a connection to Jesus of Nazareth.

Until next time, I greet you in Christ,

ENDNOTES

[1] Congregation for the Doctrine of the Faith. *Declaration 'Dominus Jesus' on the unicity and salvific universality of Jesus Christ and the Church.* Vatican City: Libreria Editrice Vaticana, 2000, p. 10.

[2] *Ibid.*, pp. 12-13.

[3] Friedman, R. E. *Who Wrote the Bible?* London: Jonathan Cape Ltd., 1987.

[4] *Für erfahrene Analytiker: Entdecken Sie die Wahrheit: Die kirchliche und staatliche Gewalt und die Gerechtigkeit Gottes.* Marktheidenfeld, Germany: Verlag DAS WORT, 2005, p. 199.

[5] Ouseley, G.J. *The Gospel of the Holy Twelve.* New edition with intro and notes, Udny, E.F. London: Kessinger Publishing, p.126.

[6] *Sonntagsblatt,* No. *17*. Munich, Apr. 24, 2005.

[7] *Catechism of the Catholic Church.* New York: Doubleday, 1995, No. 2417.

[8] Neuner, J. & Roos, H. *The Teaching of the Catholic Church as Contained in Her Documents,* edited by Rahner, K., translated by Steven, G. from the original German, *Der Glaube der Kirche.* Douglas Village, Cork, Ireland: Mercier Press, Ltd., 1967, No. 140. (printed and bound in the U.S.A. by the Pauline Fathers and Brothers Society of St. Paul at Staten Island, NY).

[9] *Ibid.,* p. 63.

[10] Tudjmann, F. *Irrwege der historischen Wahrheit.* pub.: Matica Hrvatska, 1989, p. 172.

[11] Luther, M. *Commentary on 82nd Psalm,* 1530, from: Janssen, J. *History of the German People from the Close of the Middle Ages.* A. M. Christie (trans.) St. Louis: B. Herder, 1910, Vol. X, p. 222. Available at: http://ic.net/~erasmus/RAZ247.HTM (VI. 1) (Accessed: 22 November 2006).

[12] Fischer-Wollpert, R. *Lexikon der Päpste*. Wiesbaden, Germany: Marix Verlag, 2004, p. 104.

[13] Reinhardt, V. *Rom, Kunst und Geschichte, 1480-1650*. Freiburg: Ploetz, 1992, pp. 10-16.

[14] Codex Justinianus, lib.3, tit. 12, 3, translated into English by Schaff, P. *History of the Christian Church*. Vol. 3, p. 380, New York, NY, 1994. Available at: http://www.religioustolerance.org/sabbath.htm (Accessed: 27 September 2006).

[15] Council of Laodicea, Canon XXIX. Available at: http://www.ccel.org/fathers/NPNF2-14/2ancyra/Laocns.htm (Accessed: 21 Nov. 2006).

[16] IV Lateran Council, Canon XXI. Available at: http.//www.geocities.com/Heartland/Valley/8920/churchcouncils/Ecum12.htm#On%20yearly%20confession%to%20one's%20own%20priest,%20yearly%20communion,%20the%20confessional%20seal (Accessed: 27 September 2006).

[17] *History of Canonization* [Online]. Available at: http://www.ewtn.com/JohnPaul2/cause/history.asp. (Accessed 26 Sept. 2006).

[18] Neuner, J. & Dupuis, J. *The Christian Faith in the Doctrinal Documents of the Catholic Church*. Jacques Dupuis, (ed.) St. Pauls/Alba House, Division of the Society of St. Paul, Theological Publications in India, 2001, p. 119.

[19] *Encyclopedia Britannica*. pub. H. H. Benton, Vol. 7, 1974, p. 853.

[20] Reinhardt, V. *ob. cit.,* pp. 10-16.

[21] Friedman, R. E., *ob. cit.*

[22] Lay, R. *Nachkirchliches Christentum – der lebende Jesus und die sterbende Kirche*. Düsseldorf: Econ Verlag.
Haag, H. *Upstairs, Downstairs – Did Jesus Want a Two-Class-Church?* New York: Crossroad Pub., 1998.

[23] Nigg, W. *Prophetische Denker, Löschet den Geist nicht aus,* Rottweil: Das Wort, 1986, p. 124.

[24] James, M. R. *The Apocryphal New Testament.* Oxford: Clarendon Press, 1924, pp. 8-10. Available at: http://www.earlychristianwritings.com/text/gospelebionites.html (Accessed 25 June, 2006).

[25] *Documents of Second Vatican Council, Dei verbum.* No. 11. Available at: http://www.geocities.com/Heartland/Valley/8920/churchcouncils/Ecum20.htm#4.%20On%20faith%20and%20reason (Accessed: 10 November 2006).

[26] *Jerome. The Principle Works of St. Jerome (Against Jovinianus, Book I, no. 18).* From: *Nicene and Post-Nicene Fathers, Series II, Vol. VI.* Available at: http://www.ccel.org/ccel/schaff/npnf206.vi.vi.1.html (Accessed: 5 February 2007).

[27] *The Hidden Love of Jesus for Animals: Ancient Scriptures Prove the First Christians Were Vegetarians...* Woodbridge, CT: Universal Life, the Inner Religion, 2003.

[28] *The Bible Was Falsified: Jerome, the Church Falsifier of the Bible.* Woodbridge, CT: Universal Life, the Inner Religion, 2006.

[29] Jerome. *Prefaces to Vulgate Version of New Testament: The Four Gospels.* From: *Nicene and Post-Nicene Fathers, Series II, Vol. VI.* Available at: http://www.ccel.org/ccel/schaff/npnf206/Page_488.html (Accessed: 23 November 2006).

[30] Deschner, K. *Ein Jahrhundert Heilsgeschichte.* Köln: Kiepenheuer u. W., 1982, Vol. 1, p. 25.

[31] *Spiegel, Special Edition 3/2005.* Hamburg, Germany, p. 91.

[32] Special Exposition 2005, *Mittel zum Heil, Religiöse Segens- und Schutzzeichen in der Sammlung Dr. Edward Müller.* Scientific analysis by lic. phil. Wunderlin, D. (Curator) Museum der Kulturen, Basel, Switzerland, p. 43.

[33] *Ibid.,* p. 44-45.

[34] *Ibid.*, p. 45.

[35] Deschner, K. *Der gefälschte Glaube*, Munich: Heyne, 6th ed., 1993, p. 144.

[36] *Ibid.*, p. 115.

[37] Neuner, J. & Dupuis, J. *The Christian Faith...*, p. 421.

[38] Neuner, J. & Roos, H. *Der Glaube der Kirche in den Urkunden der Lehrverkündigung.* Regensburg: Verlag Friedrich Pustet, 10. ed., 1979.

[39] *The Catholic Leader.* Brisbane, Australia, July 17, 2005.

[40] *Liber Pontificalis*, 1596, Quoted in article on papal tiara, available at:www.kath.de/kurs/vatican/tiara.php (Accessed 4 February 2007).

[41] *The Octavius of Minucius Felix,* chap. 30. Roberts, A. and Donaldson, J. (trans.) Available at: http://www.earlychristian writings.com/text/octavius.html (Accessed 22 November 2006).

[42] Eusebius, *History of the Church,* Book II, Chap. 23. Available at: http://www.newadvent.org/fathers/250102.htm (Accessed 15 September 2006).

[43] *The Clementine Homilies, (Homily 12, chap.6).* From: *The Ante-Nicene Fathers.* Rev. Roberts, A. and Donaldson, J. (editors). Vol. VIII, Grand Rapids, MI: Wm. B. Eerdmans Publishing Co., reprinted 1995. Available at: http://www.ccel. org/fathers2/ANF-08/anf08-56.htm#P4713_1392631 (Accessed 23 November 2006).

[44] Clemens of Alexandria, *Paedagogus II, 1.16: Anti-Nicene Fathers*, Translations of The Writings of the Fathers down to a.d. 325, The Rev. Roberts, A., D.D., and Donaldson, J., LL.D., (ed.). Vol. III, American reprint of Edinburgh edition, revised and chronologically arranged, with brief prefaces and occasional notes by Coxe, A. C., D.D. Edinburgh: T&T Clark, Grand Rapids, MI, Wm. B. Eerdmans Publishing Co. Available at: http://

www.ccel.org/fathers2/ANF-02/anf02-53.htm#P3706 _1120269
(Accessed: 22 November 2006).

[45] Strehlow, C. *Veganismus als Bestandteil des Christentum.* Berlin: 2000, p. 35.

[46] Chrysostom, J. *"Homily 69 on the Gospel of St. Matthew,"*
Nicene and Post-Nicene Fathers, Vol. X. Schaff, P. (ed.)
Edinburgh: T & T Clark, Grand Rapids, Michigan: Wm. B.
Eerdmans Publishing Co. Available at: http://www.ccel.org/ccel/
schaff/npnf110.iii.LXVI.html?highlight= no,streams, of,blood,
are,amongst,them,nor,cutting,up,flesh#highlight
(Accessed 21 November 2006).

[47] Eberhard, A. *Am Anfang war die Liebe, Dokumente, Briefe und
Texte der Urchristen.* Wiesbaden: Coprint, 1986, p. 162.

[48] *Ibid.,* p. 98.

[49] *Epistle of Ignatius to the Smyrnaeans,* Chap. 9, *Anti-Nicene
Fathers,* Vol 1. Available at: http://www.ccel.org/ccel/schaff/
anf01.v.vii.ix.html (Accessed: 23 November 2006).

[50] Deschner, K. *Abermals krähte der Hahn.* Düsseldorf und
Wien: Econ Verlag GmbH, 1980, p. 226f.

[51] Metzger, B. M. *The Canon of the New Testament.* Oxford:
Clarendon Press, 1987, Appendix IV, pp. 305-307.

[52] Deschner, K. *ob. cit.,* p. 200.

[53] St. Justin Martyr. *Dialogue with Trypho,* Chap. 17. Rev. Roberts, A. and Donaldson, J. (trans.)
Available at: http://www.earlychristianwritings.com/text/
justinmartyr-dialoguetrypho.html (Accessed 23 November 2006).

[54] Deschner, K. *ob. cit.,* p. 507.

[55] Leipoldt, J. *Umwelt des Urchristentums.* Berlin: Ev.
Verlagsanstalt, 5th ed., Vol. 1, 1966, p. 119.

[56] *Ibid.,* p. 121.

[57] The Saint Pachmius Orthodox Library. *Documents of the Council of Ancyra, A.D. 314, Canon 14.* Percival, H. R. (trans.) 1899. Available at: http://www.voskrese.info/spl/ancycanon.html (Accessed 23 November 2006).

[58] Parks, J. *The Conflict of the Church and the Synagogue: A Study in the Origins of Anti-Semitism.* Cleveland and New York: Meriden Books, The World Publishing Co., 1964, p. 398.

[59] *Columbia Encyclopedia,* 6th ed. New York: Columbia University Press, 2001-05. Available at: http://www.bartleby. com/65/at/AthanasSt.html (Accessed 23 November 2006).

[60] *Catechism of the Catholic Church, ob. cit.,* p. 56.

[61] The Council of Ephesus, 431. Available at: http://www.piar.hu/councils/ecum03.htm#Second% 20letter%20of%2 0Cyril%20 to %20Nestorius (Accessed 23 November 2006).

[62] Special Exposition 2005, *ob. cit.,* p. 43.

[63] Walker, B. G. *Woman's Encyclopedia of Myths and Secrets.* Harper-Collins Publishers, 1983, pp.233-234.

[64] The Council of Trent. *The canons and decrees of the sacred and ecumenical Council of Trent,* (25th Session, Decree on the invocation, veneration, and relics of saints, and on sacred images.) Waterworth, J. (ed. and trans.) London: Dolman, 1848, p. 234. Available at: http://www.geocities.com/Heartland/Valley/8920/churchcouncils/Ecum20.htm#4.%20 On%20faith %20 and %20reason (Accessed 23 November 2006).

[65] Cotterill, H. B. *Medieval Italy.* London: Geo. G. Harrap, 1915, p. 71. (*The Relics of Romanism* by Professor Arthur Noble, online article) Available at: http://www.ianpaisley.org/article.asp?Art Key=relics (Accessed 23 November 2006).

[66] Ralph Woodrow, *Babylon, Mystery Religion,* Riverside, California: 1966, p. 62. (*The Relics of Romanism...*)

[67] *The Catholic Encyclopedia,* Vol. 2, p. 661. (*The Relics of Romanism...*)

[68] This quote from the story and those following: from *Diotima, A Philosophical Review,* Vol. 2, No. 1. (Department of Philosophy, College of the Holy Cross, Worchester, Massachusetts). Available at: http://college.holycross.edu/diotima/n1v2/tolstoy. htm (Accessed 23 November 2006).

[69] Luther, M. (1537) *The Smalcald Articles.* Bente, F. and Dau, W. H. T. (trans.) Published in: *Triglot Concordia: The Symbolical Books of the Ev. Lutheran Church.* St. Louis: Concordia Publishing House, 1921, pp. 453-529. Available at: http://www. iclnet.org/pub/resources/text/wittenberg/concord/web/smc-02d. html (Accessed 25 November 2006).

[70] Ristau, K. *Concerning the Will: An historical and analytical essay examining Martin Luther's treatise "The Bondage of Will."* Quodlibet Online Journal of Christian Theology and Philosophy, Spring 2001, Vol. 3, no. 2. Available at: http://www.quodlibet. net/pdf/ristau-luther.pdf (Accessed 21 December, 2006).

[71] Luther, M. *The Bondage of Will.* Trans.: Packer, J. I. and Johnston, O. R. Grand Rapids, Michigan: Fleming H. Revell, 1957, p. 105.

[72] *Ibid.,* p. 305.

[73] *Ibid.,* p. 317.

[74] Ristau, K. *ob. cit.*

[75] *Die kirchliche und staatliche Gewalt und die Gerechtigkeit Gottes.* Marktheidenfeld, Germany: Verlag Das Wort, 2005.

[76] Ratzinger, J. *Introduction to Christianity.* Trans., Foster, J. R., trans., new preface, Miller, M. San Francisco: Ignatius Press, 2004.

[77] *Declaration on religious freedom, dignatatis humanae on the right of the person and of communities to social and civil freedom in matters religious, promulgated by his holiness Pope Paul VI, December 7, 1965, from: Decrees of the Second Vatican Council:* Available at: http://www.vatican.va/archive/hist_ coun-

cils/ii_vatican_council/documents/vat-ii_decl_19651207
_dignitatis-humanae_en.html (Accessed 26 November 2006).

[78] Jaspers, K. *Der philosophische Glaube,* 9th ed., 1988, p. 73.

[79] Dostoyevski, F. *The Brothers Karamazov.* New York:
New American Library of World Literature, Inc.,1960, p. 237.

[80] *The Great Cosmic Teachings of Jesus of Nazareth for His
Apostles and Disciples Who Could Understand Them.*
Marktheidenfeld, Germany: Verlag Das Wort, 1999.

[81] *Guardian Unlimited.* April 24, 2005. Available at: http://
observer.guardian.co.uk/international/story/0,6903, 1469055,
00.html (Accessed 26 November 2006).

The following books can be ordered directly:
www.Universal-Spirit.cc.
1-800-846-2691

Universal Life
The Inner Religion
P.O. Box 3549
Woodbridge, CT 06525

Universal Life
P.O. Box 5643
97006 Würzburg
Germany

Books by Gabriele, the prophetess of God

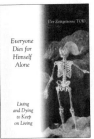

The Contemporary DEATH
Everyone Dies for Himself Alone
Living and Dying to Keep on Living

The contents of this book are relevant for every person who wants to get away from the fear of death and grow into a conscious life, into a sense of security, a peace of mind and inner steadfastness. For: "Whoever learns to understand his life, need no longer fear death." The reader of this book will find explanations and insight into the until now unknown correlations between life and death, into the condition and health of the soul under the many different circumstances surrounding the process of dying and about what awaits the soul in the beyond once the physical body passes away.

160 p., Order No. S 368 en, ISBN: 978-1-890841-48-5 / 1-890841-48-X

Cause and Development
of All Illness
What a person sows, he will reap

What philosophers and scientists have tried unsuccessfully to figure out over millenia is revealed in this book, directly from the divine-spiritual world: The emergence of the material universe, the correlations between spirit and matter, the interchange between soul and body, and so on. Beyond this, a fullness of previously unknown details is given about the frontier regions between spirit and matter, about the development and

Cause and Development
of All Illness

emergence of human beings, about the course of events set in motion by human beings through their interaction with their fellow man and with the forces of nature, about the power of thought in the life of the individual and his surroundings, about details that are given on the past, present and future of the earth and much, much more. An exciting and fascinating reading!

340 p., Order No. S 117 en, ISBN 978-890841-37-9 / 890841-37-4

The Living Word of God for our Time

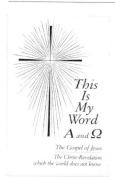

This Is My Word
A and Ω
The Gospel of Jesus
The Christ Revelation,
which true Christians the world over
have come to know

A book that lets you really get to know about Jesus, the Christ, about the truth of his activity and life as Jesus of Nazareth. From the contents: The falsification of the teachings of Jesus of Nazareth during the past 2000 years - Pharisees, yesterday and today - Jesus loved the animals and always supported them - The meaning and purpose of life on earth - God does not punish or castigate. The law of cause and effect - The teaching of "eternal damnation" is a mockery of God - Life after the death of the body - Equality between men and women - The coming times ...

1078 p., Order No. S 007 en, ISBN: 978-890841-38-6 / 1-890841-38-2

The All-Spirit, GOD,
Speaks Directly Into Our Time
Through His Prophetess

He does not speak the word of the Bible

14 divine revelations given from 1987 to 1997 have been put together in this volume. What is remarkable about this collections of revelations is their often full relevance to the explosive events of today's time. For example, about current events on the world's stage, about the intolerable conditions on the earth, the abuse of the teachings of Jesus, the Christ, by the institutional churches and much, much more. As no other, this book conveys the nearness of God and His deep love for each one of His children. An exciting read for truth-seekers regardless of religion, race or nationality.

256 p., Order No. S 137 en, ISBN: 978-1-890841-36-2 / 1-890841-36-6